Aircraft

WARWICK PRESS

CONTENTS

Author   Brian Williams
Editor   Michael Dempsey

Library of Congress Cataloging in Publication Data

Williams, Brian.
   Aircraft.

   (Modern knowledge library)
   Includes index.

   SUMMARY: Discusses various kinds of aircraft including their history, design, and construction.

   1. Aeronautics—Juvenile literature.   2. Airplanes—Juvenile literature.   [1. Aeronautics.   2. Airplanes]   I. Title

TL547.W63   629.133   76–13645
ISBN 0–531–02440–7
ISBN 0–531–01195–X lib. bdg.

First published in Great Britain by Sampson Low in 1974
Printed in Great Britain by Purnell & Sons, Ltd,
Paulton (Avon) and London
6 5 4 3 2 1

Aircraft

Since earliest times men have wanted to fly like birds. They made wings and flapped them. They jumped from towers. But their muscles were far too weak to lift their bodies into the air. Man's first success in the air came not through wings but from balloons. The story of the balloon started in the eighteenth century when two men found out that a bag filled with hot air would rise. It ended with the vast but ill-fated airships of the 1930s.

Meanwhile, in the nineteenth century, the way that a kite rises was used to make a glider. And by the end of that century powered flight awaited only the light-weight engine. In December, 1903, man's dream came true with the Wright brothers' flight over the sands at Kitty Hawk. Now, little more than seventy years later, over one million people are whisked around the world each day. They travel at speeds undreamed of by the early pioneers in planes that grow ever larger.

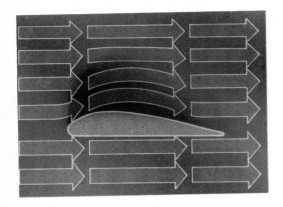

The Science of Flight

Why does an aircraft, which is heavier than air, stay up? The answer lies in the forces which act on an aircraft in flight.

The shape of the wing is called an *aerofoil*. The wing is curved at the top and flat at the bottom. Air passing over the top surface (shown by the direction of the arrows) travels faster than air beneath. This is because it has further to go. As a result, the air pressure above the wing is less than the air pressure below. This gives a suction effect on the wing and lifts it. Additional lift is produced by the slower air flowing under the wing, which pushes up on the wing.

It is possible to show the flow of air around a model in a wind tunnel. Wind tunnel tests show how a wing design will perform at different speeds.

An aircraft stays in the air because of the *lift* caused by the movement of the wings through air. The wing of an aircraft has a special shape, known as an *aerofoil*. It is curved at the top and flat at the bottom. Air passing over the top surface travels faster than air beneath because it has further to go. This means that the air pressure above the wing is less than the air pressure below it. The upward suction produced in this way lifts the wing. The lift is increased by tilting the wing upward slightly at the front.

There are four forces which act on an aircraft. The first is lift. To produce lift, the wings must move through the air at high speed. So the aircraft needs a second force, or *thrust*, to propel it forward. This thrust is supplied either by a propeller or by a jet.

As the thrust drives the aircraft forward, another force, known as *drag*, holds it back. This drag is caused by the air as the aircraft moves through it. The fourth force which acts on an aircraft in flight is its own weight. The aircraft would fall to earth, were it not for the lift given by the wings.

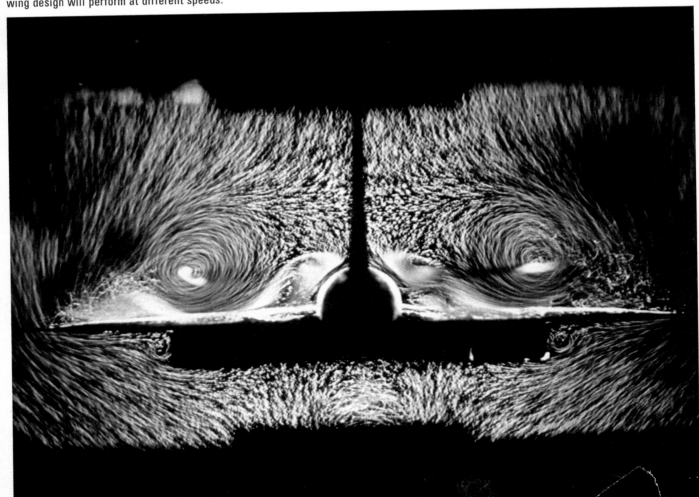

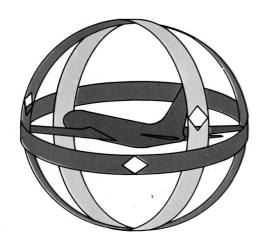

Above: An aircraft in flight can move in three directions. "Pitch" is movement of the nose up and down. "Yaw" is a slewing from side to side. "Roll" is a dipping of the wings up and down. Below: The upward slope of each wing from the body of the aircraft is known as the "dihedral". It helps to correct a roll. In level flight both wings give equal lift. If a gust of wind should tilt one wing, the aircraft rolls, and slips sideways. This causes extra airflow under the lowered wing, and this extra lift corrects the tilt.

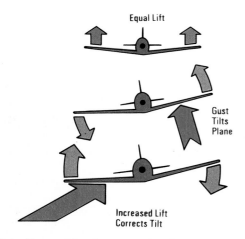

Equal Lift

Gust Tilts Plane

Increased Lift Corrects Tilt

Right: To control and steer an aircraft the pilot has two main controls. These are the rudder bar and the control column. The rudder bar has two foot pedals connected to the rudder. This is a flap on the tailplane which moves from side to side. As it moves, the airflow pushes against it and this causes the aircraft to turn. As the rudder moves left, the tail is pushed to the right and the aircraft makes a left turn. The control column is joined to the elevators (flaps on the tail) and the ailerons (flaps on the back edge of the wing). When the elevators are angled downwards, more air pushes up against them. This pressure pushes up the tail and the aircraft dives. By moving the ailerons up or down, the pilot can roll the aircraft to left or right. This is necessary when turning, for the aircraft must be "banked" to prevent it skidding through the air.

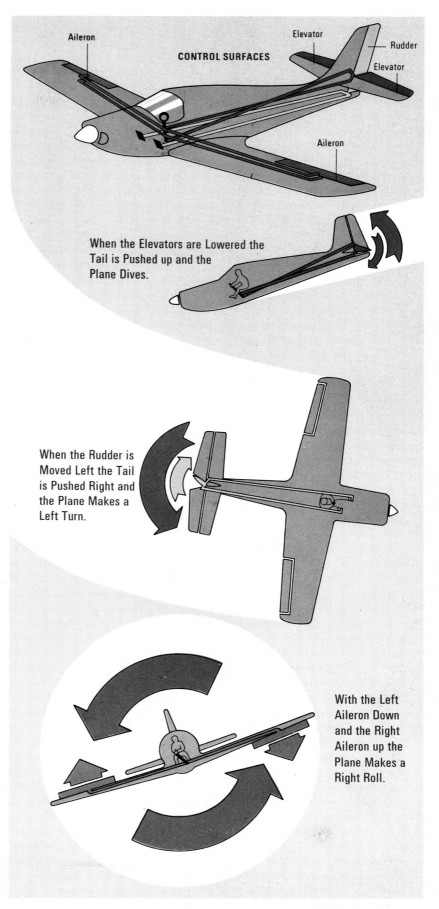

CONTROL SURFACES

Aileron

Elevator

Rudder

Elevator

Aileron

When the Elevators are Lowered the Tail is Pushed up and the Plane Dives.

When the Rudder is Moved Left the Tail is Pushed Right and the Plane Makes a Left Turn.

With the Left Aileron Down and the Right Aileron up the Plane Makes a Right Roll.

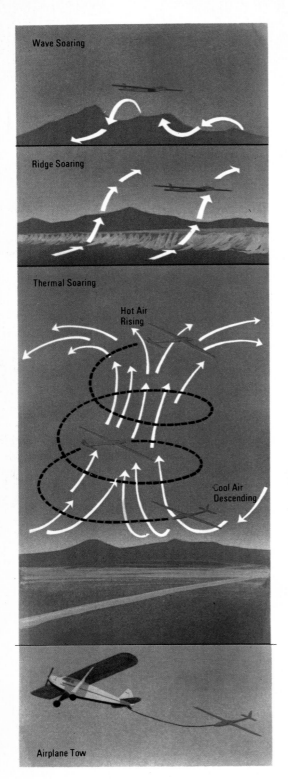

Wave Soaring

Ridge Soaring

Thermal Soaring

Hot Air Rising

Cool Air Descending

Airplane Tow

A glider soars by finding rising currents of air. A range of hills can shoot air upwards in a wave-like pattern. This is called "wave soaring". Winds blowing against a ridge or cliff give a similar effect and this is known as "ridge soaring". A glider can also soar inside a current of warm rising air known as a thermal. A favorite way of launching is to use a light plane to tow the glider aloft.

Gliders and Gliding

The soaring glider has no engine to keep it aloft. It is perhaps man's nearest approach to the graceful flight of birds.

Any aircraft can fly without using its engine, provided it can go fast enough to give enough lift. This it can do by diving. A glider, which has no engine, stays aloft by diving at a very flat angle. It makes the best use of the lift from its wings. Gliders have long wings, to increase this amount of lift, and their fuselages (bodies) are streamlined to reduce drag. Once a glider has gained height, it can stay up for a long time.

But how does a glider become airborne in the first place? It has to be launched from the ground, and this is done in a number of ways. One way is to use a powered aircraft as a tug to tow the glider until it has gained enough height. The tow line is then released and the glider is free. Other ways of launching are similar to the way you launch a kite by running into the wind. A line is attached to the glider. Then either a moving truck or a winch is used to pull the glider up into the air.

Soaring

Once launched, a glider should only be able to fly downwards. But it can soar, or gain height, by finding currents of warm air which are rising. Such currents are known as "thermals". Once he has found a

Towed gliders were used in World War II to carry troops. The glider was towed to the target and then released to make a landing. Allied glider troops were landed across the Rhine in the greatest airborne attack of the war.

thermal, the glider pilot can circle within it and spiral upwards in the rising air. After a while, as it rises, the air cools and the glider has to find another thermal. Soaring can also be done above hills. Winds blowing against a ridge cause rising currents of air in which a glider can fly backwards and forwards. In ideal conditions, gliders can soar so high that the pilot needs oxygen and even a special flying suit.

A glider soars high above its airfield. The steep slope at the end of the airfield provides an upward air current ideal for gliding.

The History of Gliding

The first gliders were models, built by the early pioneers of flying. Sir George Cayley built a model glider in 1804 and flew a full scale man-carrying glider in 1853. The German Otto Lilienthal made many flights in bat-like gliders. He hung from these and controlled the machine by swinging his body. Lilienthal was killed gliding, but interest in his work continued. He showed the way to powered flight. The Wright brothers started by building gliders. They experimented with wing shapes, until they had a successful man-carrying glider. This was followed by the powered "Flyer" of 1903.

During the 1930s interest in gliders revived. They were flown for sport in Germany. Troop-carrying gliders, first developed by the Germans, were used during World War II. Gliding is now a popular sport, with many competitions.

Otto Lilienthal controlled his gliders by swinging his body. Lilienthal was killed gliding in 1896 after more than 2,000 flights.

7

Balloons and Airships

The discovery that a paper bag filled with hot air would rise led to the first successful flying machines — balloons and airships.

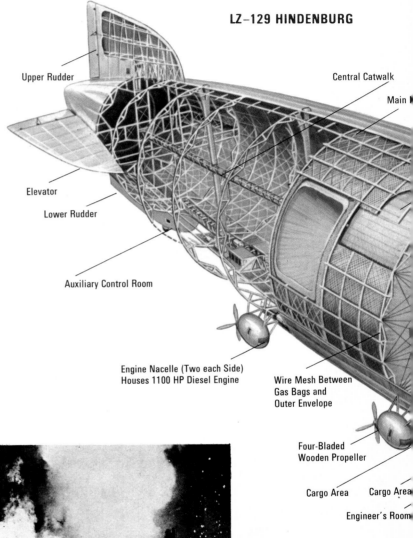

At 804 feet long the "Hindenburg" would have dwarfed even the Boeing 747 (231 feet).

LZ-129 HINDENBURG

Upper Rudder

Central Catwalk

Main

Elevator

Lower Rudder

Auxiliary Control Room

Engine Nacelle (Two each Side) Houses 1100 HP Diesel Engine

Wire Mesh Between Gas Bags and Outer Envelope

Four-Bladed Wooden Propeller

Cargo Area   Cargo Area

Engineer's Room

In France in 1783 the brothers Joseph and Etienne Montgolfier found that if they filled a paper bag with hot air it would rise. They worked with silk bags before building a full size balloon. The hot air came from a brazier burning in the basket beneath the balloon. The first manned balloon flight took place in Paris in 1783. The brave balloonists were Jean-Francois Pilatre de Rozier and the Marquis d'Arlandes, who flew over five miles in a Montgolfier balloon. Later that year J. A. C. Charles flew for an hour and threequarters in a balloon filled with hydrogen gas.

In 1785 the Frenchman J. P. Blanchard and the American John Jeffries flew the English Channel in a balloon.

The disadvantage of balloons was that they could not be steered. They drifted with the winds. Sails, oars and even hand-driven paddle wheels were tried without success.

In 1852 Henri Giffard built a hydrogen balloon powered by a small steam engine driving a propeller. This was the

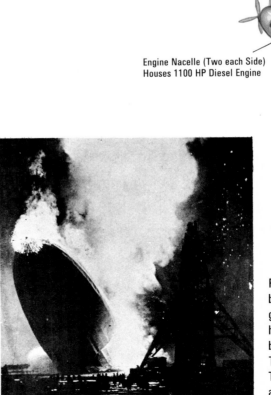

Far left: A modern hot-air balloon. These balloons carry gas cylinders to provide the heat. Hot-air ballooning has become a popular sport. Left: The end of the "Hindenburg". This was also the end of the airship.

first true "airship". Electric motors were also tried. The first man to fly an airship powered by a gasoline engine was the Brazilian pioneer Alberto Santos-Dumont in 1898.

The first airships were known as "dirigibles", from a French word meaning "steerable". Most were not rigid. The cigar-shaped gas bag was kept in shape by the pressure of gas inside. Once punctured, the whole ship collapsed. Rigid airships had a fabric skin stretched over an aluminum framework. Inside the framework were a number of gas bags. Rigid airships kept their shape even when empty.

The most successful rigid airships were those built in Germany by Count Ferdinand von Zeppelin. The first Zeppelin flew in 1900. Zeppelins made the first passenger-carrying services and during World War I were used to bomb England.

After the war it seemed the huge passenger airship might challenge the airplane. Germany, Britain and the United States built large airships in the 1920s and 1930s. Largest of all was the Zeppelin *Hindenburg* which carried people across the Atlantic in luxury. It had a lounge complete with grand piano.

But airships had many drawbacks. Some were filled with helium, a gas that cannot catch fire. But most used the lighter but highly inflammable gas hydrogen. They were also difficult to handle in bad weather. Many airships were lost in accidents. In 1937 the *Hindenburg* burst into flames while mooring and 36 people lost their lives. This disaster was the end of the airship.

The Montgolfiers' balloon. The balloonists had to stoke a fire to produce the hot air. They had to throw water on the fabric to prevent disaster.

J. P. Blanchard and John Jeffries crossed the English Channel in 1785 in a hydrogen balloon. It had a rudder and "oars".

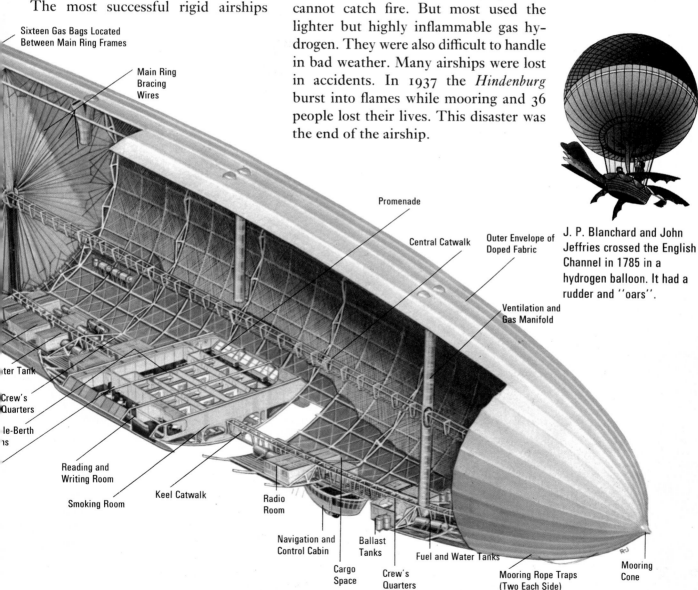

Sixteen Gas Bags Located Between Main Ring Frames

Main Ring Bracing Wires

Promenade

Central Catwalk

Outer Envelope of Doped Fabric

Ventilation and Gas Manifold

ter Tank

Crew's Quarters

le-Berth
ns

Reading and Writing Room

Smoking Room

Keel Catwalk

Radio Room

Navigation and Control Cabin

Ballast Tanks

Cargo Space

Crew's Quarters

Fuel and Water Tanks

Mooring Rope Traps (Two Each Side)

Mooring Cone

The First Flight

The air age began on December 17, 1903 with a wobbling flight of 120 feet over the sands of Kitty Hawk, North Carolina.

The Wright Brothers, Wilbur (1867–1912) and Orville (1871–1948), were bicycle makers from Dayton, Ohio. In 1900 they built a full-size glider and made a number of brief flights. Their work resulted in the world's first powered flight.

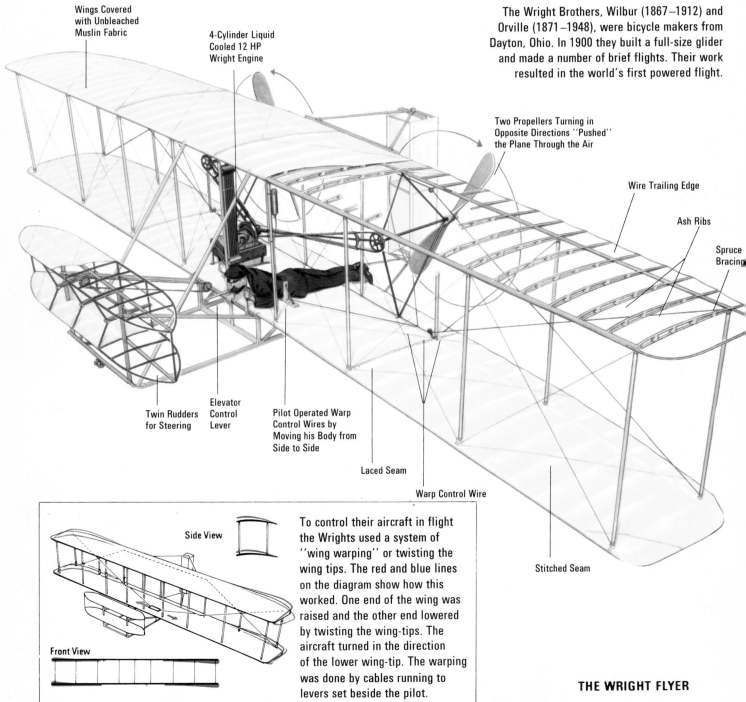

Wings Covered with Unbleached Muslin Fabric

4-Cylinder Liquid Cooled 12 HP Wright Engine

Two Propellers Turning in Opposite Directions "Pushed" the Plane Through the Air

Wire Trailing Edge

Ash Ribs

Spruce Bracing

Twin Rudders for Steering

Elevator Control Lever

Pilot Operated Warp Control Wires by Moving his Body from Side to Side

Laced Seam

Warp Control Wire

Stitched Seam

Side View

Front View

To control their aircraft in flight the Wrights used a system of "wing warping" or twisting the wing tips. The red and blue lines on the diagram show how this worked. One end of the wing was raised and the other end lowered by twisting the wing-tips. The aircraft turned in the direction of the lower wing-tip. The warping was done by cables running to levers set beside the pilot.

THE WRIGHT FLYER

From earliest times man dreamed of flying. He watched birds soaring in the sky and longed to do the same. From time to time people tried to imitate birds. They jumped from cliffs and towers with wings strapped to their arms. All the attempts failed. Arm muscles are far too weak to lift a man from the ground.

In the 1700s man succeeded in becoming airborne using hot-air and hydrogen balloons. But the story of true powered flight began in the early 1800s. The English scientist, Sir George Cayley, saw how a kite develops "lift" when held in a stream of air. In 1804 he built a successful model glider. This was just a kite on a five-foot pole with an adjustable tail at the end. In 1853, Cayley built a glider which flew across a small valley carrying his coachman. The fact that a wing would support a man in the air was finally proved by the German, Otto Lilienthal. He built a number of gliders and made

The Henson Aerial Steam Carriage. Designed in 1842 this steam-powered aircraft never flew. It was too heavy and under-powered.

A monoplane built by Felix du Temple (1823–1890) made a powered "hop" in about 1874.

On December 17, 1903 the Wright Flyer made the world's first powered flight with Orville at the controls and Wilbur running alongside. The machine was airborne for 12 seconds and flew 120 feet.

The Eole designed by Clement Ader (1841–1925) did manage a short flight in 1890. It had a 20 hp steam engine.

more than 2000 glides between 1891 and 1896.

The big problem facing the pioneers of the 1800s was to find a way of powering their craft. At that time the steam engine was the only choice, but it was too heavy for use in aircraft. Many steam-powered aircraft were designed, and some were built. But the most successful full-scale models made only brief hops. These included a four-ton plane built in England by the American inventor Sir Hiram Maxim, and the batlike *Avion III* tested in France in 1897 by Clement Ader.

The invention of the gasoline engine paved the way to powered flight. In the United States, Samuel Pierpoint Langley built a gasoline-engined model, *Aerodrome*, which flew in 1901. On December 7 and 8, 1903, the full-size *Aerodrome* was launched twice over the Potomac River. Each time, the machine fell into the river. Nine days later, Orville Wright made the first powered flight at Kitty Hawk, North Carolina. The Wright Flyer, powered by a 12 horsepower engine, flew 120 feet in front of five witnesses. The dream of flight had come true.

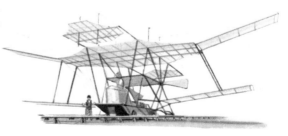

Sir Hiram Maxim (1840–1916) built this huge twin-engined biplane in 1894. It did manage to lift itself from the railroad track on which it was launched. But it never flew in the true sense.

Pioneer Planes

The Wright brothers' success encouraged other aircraft pioneers. Before long many strange looking craft were taking to the air.

After the historic flight in their first "Flyer", the Wright brothers built two more machines. The "Flyer No. 3" was the world's first fully steerable aircraft. It could fly a figure of eight and stay in the air for 30 minutes. All the Wright's machines had to be constantly controlled by the pilot. He had to use elevators and a system of wing "warping", or twisting, for turns. This warping arrangement was later replaced by ailerons.

Pioneers in Europe

The first Europeans to follow the Wrights were not very successful. In 1905 Gabriel Voisin and Louis Blériot tried without success to launch two biplane gliders. Not until 1906 was the first heavier-than-air flight made in Europe. It was made by the Brazilian Santos-Dumont in a kite-like flying machine.

France soon became the aviation center of Europe. In 1907 Louis Blériot designed and flew a monoplane which showed the way for aircraft of the future. In 1908 Henry Farman won a prize of 50,000 francs for a round flight of almost one mile in a Voisin biplane. Leon Levavasseur built the *Antoinette*, a monoplane with many improvements. In July, 1909 Louis Blériot flew the English Channel. And in August of the same year the first-ever air races were held at Rheims, France. The only American competitor was Glenn Curtiss who won the Gordon Bennett speed trophy in his *Golden Flyer*. No fewer than a quarter of a million people attended the Rheims meeting. This showed the tremendous

The 14-bis of Alberto Santos-Dumont made the first airplane flight in Europe. This strange-looking machine had the tail in the front. It looked as if it were flying backwards.

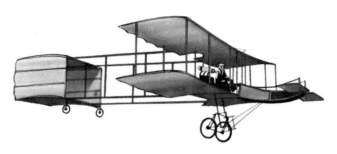

The Voisin brothers Gabriel and Charles were the world's first commercial aircraft makers. The Voisin "Bird of Passage" (1909) was one of their successful flying machines.

Henry Farman improved the Voisin design. His Type III Biplane first flew in 1909 and won the London to Manchester prize in 1910.

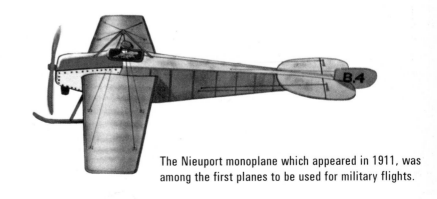

The Nieuport monoplane which appeared in 1911, was among the first planes to be used for military flights.

interest that had grown in aviation.

The first twin-engined planes soon appeared. Some of them had one engine in front of the pilot and the other behind. In 1911 Glenn Curtiss flew the world's first seaplane. Two years later in Russia Igor Sikorsky built the first four-engined airplanes. Airmail was carried for the first time and a few brave passengers were carried into the skies.

Many of the early airplanes were strange to our eyes. Some, like Santos-Dumont's 14-*bis*, looked as if they were flying backwards. Pilots often had to lie face down. Some engines were "pushers" (with propellers facing backwards) and others were "tractors" (with propellers facing forwards). But the most successful design to emerge from the pioneer days was the sturdy double-winged aircraft – the biplane. It was built of a wood framework covered with fabric and with an engine mounted at the front.

However, the airplane was still little more than a toy for use in exhibitions and for sport.

The "Golden Flyer" was designed by Glenn Curtiss. It won the speed trophy at the Rheims air festival in 1909.

Louis Blériot flew across the English Channel in just over 30 minutes. He landed in a field behind Dover Castle.

Blériot in his monoplane before take-off from the cliffs near Calais on July 25, 1909. The aircraft weighed just over 660 pounds and had a speed of around 41 miles an hour.

World War I

World War I speeded up progress in aircraft design. Air forces came into being and the legend of the "fighter ace" was born.

The United States, Germany, Britain, France, Russia and Italy all had airplanes in military service before World War I. However, the generals thought airplanes were useful only as flying observation posts.

At the start of the war aircraft flew over the lines unarmed. The pilots waved cheerfully at each other. But soon it was realized that some effort should be made to stop the enemy planes. Pilots exchanged pistol shots at first, but later machine guns were fitted. It was a French pilot, Roland Garros, who discovered a way of firing a machine-gun right through his whirling propeller blades. He fitted metal plates to the blades to protect them. Anthony Fokker, a Dutch designer working for Germany, improved upon this idea. He linked the machine-gun trigger to the engine in such a way that the gun was only fired when the propeller blades were out of the way. Soon, aerial "dog fights" took place. The leading pilots, the "aces", became national heroes.

The bomber too was developed for attacks on the enemy. Ger-

Top to bottom: The French Spad, British SE5 and American Curtiss Jenny. These were three of the most successful aircraft of the war. The Spad and the SE5 were fighters. Several thousand Curtiss Jennies were built as training aircraft.

An aerial dog-fight between a British Sopwith Camel and a German Fokker D VII (perhaps the finest fighter to appear in the war). At first aircraft bore no markings to show whose side they were on. Later the opposing forces painted markings on the wings, fuselage and tail. The pilots who fought one another in the air admired each other's courage. There were many examples of chivalry.

14

man Gotha bombers raided London and the British replied with raids by planes such as the Handley Page 0/400. Seaplanes were developed and deck landings were made on ships at sea.

Airships were used against submarines as well as for bombing raids. And for the first time civilians were exposed to the dangers of war by attacks from the air.

There were new tactics for air warfare. Formation flying replaced the one-against-one fights of the early days. By the end of the war the airplane had become an important weapon. Special types had been designed for different jobs. Experts foresaw that the warplane would play an even more important part in future wars.

Three of the fighter "aces" of World War I. From left to right: Guynemer (France), von Richthofen (Germany) and Albert Ball (Britain). Von Richthofen, with 80 "kills" was the leading German ace and the "flying circus" of the so-called "red Baron" became famous.

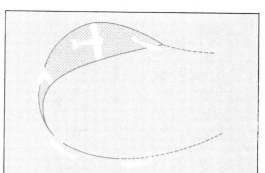

Various maneuvers were used by pilots to enable them to change direction quickly. One of the most famous aerobatic maneuvers was the Immelmann Turn. This consisted of a half loop and roll off the top. It was invented by the German fighter ace Max Immelmann.

Epic Flights

After the war brave fliers opened new air routes. They proved that the airplane was a useful means of transport.

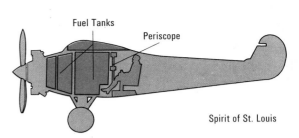

Fuel Tanks

Periscope

Spirit of St. Louis

From the earliest days of flying, prizes were offered for record-breaking flights. An English newspaper, the *Daily Mail*, had offered £1,000 for the first flight across the English Channel. This was won in 1909 by Blériot. The same newspaper offered £10,000 for the first crossing of the Atlantic Ocean. After the end of World War I, this prize had not been won. In May 1919 a Curtiss NC–4 flying boat of the United States Navy made a flight from the United States to England. It stopped on the way at Newfoundland, the Azores and Portugal. But the winners of the *Daily Mail* prize, and the first men to fly the Atlantic non-stop were two Royal Air Force officers, Captain John Alcock and Lieutenant Arthur Whitten-Brown. In a converted Vickers Vimy bomber, a twin engined biplane, Alcock and Brown flew from Newfoundland to Ireland in June 1919. Their flight of

Charles Lindbergh was born in 1902. He learned his flying as an airmail pilot flying from St. Louis to Chicago. His solo flight made people realize the value of the airplane.

Right: Captain John Alcock. Far right: Lieutenant Arthur Whitten-Brown.

Lindbergh's Ryan monoplane "Spirit of St. Louis" was powered by a 237 hp Wright J-5C Whirlwind nine-cylinder radial engine. With its fuel tanks full to the brim for the long flight across the Atlantic, the "Spirit of St. Louis" had a maximum speed of 124 miles an hour and a range of 4,650 miles. Lindbergh carried no radio, parachute or sextant in order to save weight. The "Spirit of St. Louis" was a flying fuel tank. The only way that Lindbergh could see ahead was through a periscope. This was one of the great epic flights.

Below: The Vickers Vimy of Alcock and Brown after their Atlantic crossing in June 1919. The Vimy, a World War I bomber, first flew in 1917. Its top speed was 103 miles an hour and the machine used by Alcock and Brown had a range of 2,440 miles. The trans-Atlantic flight was made in appalling weather. It ended in a peat bog at Clifden, Ireland.

1,960 miles lasted just under 16½ hours.

Other record-breaking flights followed. The brave pilots and their aircraft became famous. Their flights were followed with great excitement.

Solo Across the Atlantic

A prize was offered for the first non-stop flight from New York to Paris. This prize was won in May 1927 by Charles Lindbergh. His flight was one of the greatest single feats in the history of aviation. Piloting his Ryan monoplane *Spirit of St. Louis*, Lindbergh flew east. He battled against the wind, the cold and his ever increasing weariness. He reached Le Bourget near Paris on May 21, after a flight of 3,600 miles, lasting 33 hours and 31 minutes.

Other famous flights followed. In the same year, 1927, Maitland and Hegenberger of the United States flew from California to Hawaii. In 1928 a German Junkers flew the North Atlantic from east to west. Amelia Earhart flew the Atlantic alone in 1932, and that year Jim Mollison made the first east to west solo flight.

Wings Around the World

The first round-the-world flight, took place as early as 1924. Four American Douglas biplanes made short hops from one fueling point to the next. Two planes finished the trip, which lasted 175 days. In 1931 Wiley Post and Harold Gatty in a monoplane, the *Winnie Mae*, flew round the world in 8 days 16 hours. Two years later Post circled the world alone in the same plane in under eight days. By 1938 Howard Hughes, in a twin-engined Lockheed, was able to circle the world in less than four days. But by this time, the airliner had become fast and efficient. The days of the epic flight were coming to an end. The world's first modern airliner, the Boeing 247, appeared in 1933. The year 1936 saw the Douglas DC-3, the world's most successful airliner. Well over 10,000 were built and many still fly.

Above: Amelia Earhart (left) was the first woman to cross the Atlantic by air. In 1928 she flew as a passenger in a Fokker monoplane from Newfoundland to Wales. Four years later she flew the Atlantic solo in a Lockheed Vega. She disappeared over the South Pacific in 1937. Commander Richard E. Byrd (above, right) flew over both Poles and made one of the first Atlantic crossings.

Wiley Post was another pilot whose flights made him world famous. After his round-the-world flight, Post received a ticker-tape welcome in New York. His flights proved the value of navigational instruments. Wiley Post was killed in a crash near Pt. Barrow, Alaska, in 1935.

Left: Amy Johnson was the first woman to fly solo from England to Australia. She later made a number of records for long-distance flights.

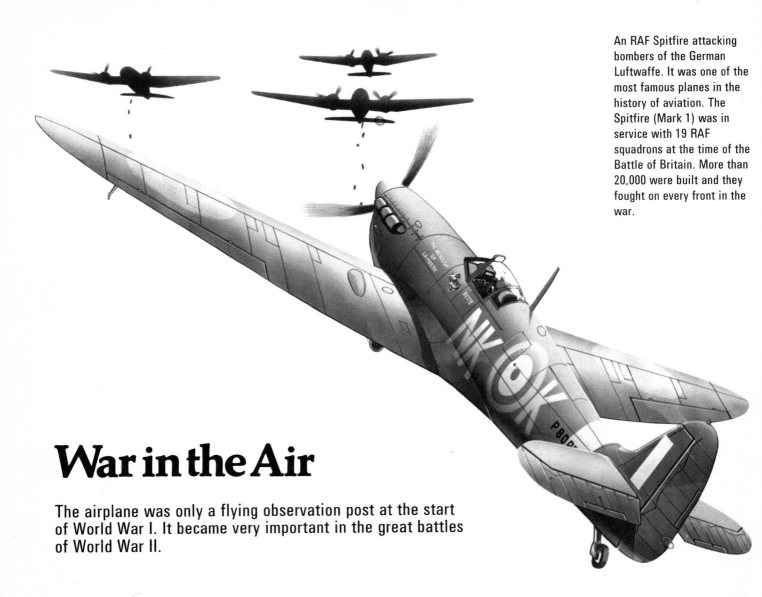

An RAF Spitfire attacking bombers of the German Luftwaffe. It was one of the most famous planes in the history of aviation. The Spitfire (Mark 1) was in service with 19 RAF squadrons at the time of the Battle of Britain. More than 20,000 were built and they fought on every front in the war.

War in the Air

The airplane was only a flying observation post at the start of World War I. It became very important in the great battles of World War II.

WORLD WAR II INSIGNIA

UK   USSR   Japan

USA   Germany

When war broke out in 1939 the German air force, the Luftwaffe, was a deadly force. Fighters, dive bombers and bombers were used to blast a way through defenses and support the army. The Germans also began the use of paratroops, which they used in their invasion of Crete.

Control of the air was needed for victory. For that reason the Battle of Britain which began in August 1940 was a turning point in the war. It was a battle fought in the air between the Luftwaffe and the British Royal Air Force. Losses of machines and men were heavy on both sides. But the Luftwaffe did not win in the sky, so the plan to invade Britain was abandoned.

In the Pacific the importance of air power was again shown. Japanese carrier-based aircraft bombed Pearl Harbor on December 7, 1941. They sank five US battleships in a little over an hour. Following this, the Japanese and US navies fought mostly at long range, using aircraft from carriers.

In 1939 fighters had only a short range and could not fight far from their bases. But the Allies developed long-range fighters to

Smoke pours from a crippled US battleship after the Japanese attack on Pearl Harbor on December 7, 1941. Fortunately for the Allies, the US carriers normally based at Pearl Harbor were at sea when the Japanese attacked.

escort bombers. Heavy bombers, such as the Lancaster, B–17 and B–29, were used in large numbers to bomb German cities.

In the end Allied air power won the day. The Germans made the world's first jet plane, the Me262, and the first rocket plane, the Me163. But these came too late in the war. Piston-engined aircraft were improved. By 1945, for example, the Spitfires were 100 miles an hour faster than the 1939 models. Other great fighters of the war were the American Thunderbolt and Mustang, the British Hurricane and Typhoon, the German Me109 and Focke-Wulf 190, and the Japanese Zero.

Jet Planes and Radar

The war advanced aviation in many ways. The coming of jet aircraft was a sign of things to come. Equally important was the invention of radar, first used in Britain in 1940. At that time radar was used to track enemy planes from the ground. It played an important part in the Battle of Britain. When the war ended, radar was fitted in airliners.

P-51 Mustang

The North American P-51 Mustang was the most famous fighter used by the United States during World War II. It was used as a long-range fighter to accompany the daylight bombers of the USAF on raids over Germany. The Mustang had a top speed of more than 430 miles per hour. With its long range and speed, the Mustang was one of the most successful warplanes ever.

Hawker Hurricane

The Hawker Hurricane first flew in 1935. At the beginning of the war the RAF had about 300 in service. The sturdy eight-gun Hurricane was important in the Battle of Britain. Its 1030 hp Rolls-Royce engine gave it a top speed of about 330 miles an hour. More than 14,000 Hurricanes were built.

Messerschmitt Bf 109

The Messerschmitt Bf 109 first entered Luftwaffe service in 1937. The fighter was used by German pilots in the Spanish Civil War of 1936–39. The Bf 109 was used throughout the war. Armed with machine guns and cannon, the Bf 109E had a top speed of 357 miles per hour. As with other fighters of World War II, the Bf 109 was improved. Later models were faster and more heavily armed.

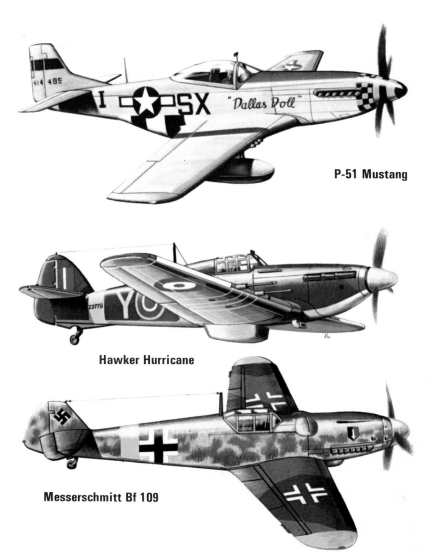

P-51 Mustang

Hawker Hurricane

Messerschmitt Bf 109

The Jet Age

The jet age brought speeds undreamed of by the early pioneers.

In a turboprop engine hot gases give jet thrust and also drive an ordinary propeller. The flow of air through the compressor and then the combustion chamber is shown by the arrows.

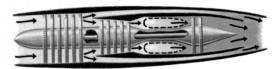

In a turbojet engine air is sucked in at the front. After it is compressed the air goes to the combustion chamber where fuel is burned. The hot exhaust gases give jet thrust.

In a bypass "turbofan" engine the blades of the front (low pressure) compressor are lengthened to form a fan. The fan pushes in extra air, bypassing the combustion chamber, and a more powerful, quieter engine results.

The simplest form of jet engine is the ramjet. It has no compressor and only works properly at high speed. Air is "rammed" into the combustion chamber by the forward motion of the engine.

The jet engine is quite simple. For every force there is an equal force in the opposite direction. This is known as a "reaction" force. When air is forced backwards at high speed, a powerful reaction force is produced. You can see this for yourself by letting go a blown up balloon. As the air rushes out, the balloon flies in the opposite direction.

From earliest times inventors tried water jets and steam jets. But the true jet engine was not invented until the 1930s. Engineers knew that piston engines do not work very well above certain heights because the air is too thin. And propellers will not work above about 500 miles an hour because of air resistance. The answer was an engine with no pistons and no propellers.

An RAF officer, Frank Whittle, patented a design for a jet engine in 1930. But the first jet plane to fly was the German Heinkel He 178, which was tested in 1939. Whittle's engine was first flown in 1941 in the Gloster/Whittle E28/39. But only two jet aircraft, the German Messerschmitt Me262 and the British Gloster Meteor, saw service in World War II. The jet was too late to play an important role in the war. But after 1945 jet aircraft swiftly took the place of piston-engined aircraft. The first four-jet bomber was the American Boeing B–47.

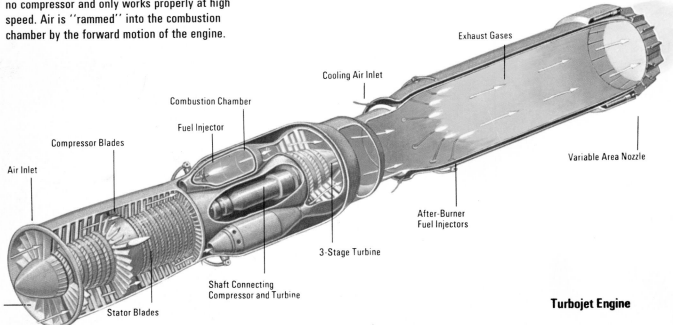

Turbojet Engine

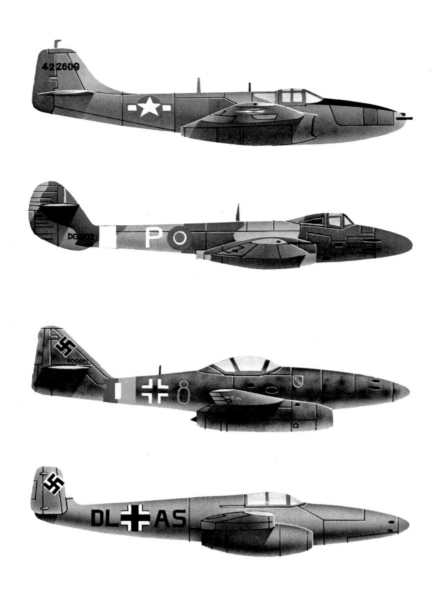

Below: The Rolls-Royce RB-211 is a powerful jet engine. It develops 45,000 pounds of thrust.

How the Jet Engine Works

A propeller works by pushing a large amount of air backwards. A jet engine pushes a thin column of air backwards at very high speed. A turbojet engine has a compressor, a combustion chamber and a turbine. Air is sucked in at the front, compressed (squeezed) and mixed with fuel in the combustion chamber. This produces a stream of hot gas which is passed through the blades of a turbine. The turbine spins and drives the compressor. The hot gas rushes out of the jet's tailplane. This backwards force produces an equal but opposite reaction force. So the engine, and the aircraft, travel forwards.

Different types of jet engine have been made for different jobs. The turboprop engine is a mixture of the jet and the propeller. The turbine drives an ordinary propeller as well as the compressor. By reversing the jet's thrust, so that the exhaust gases travel forwards, a plane can be slowed quickly after it has touched down.

The 'Jumbo' Jets

Between 1960 and 1970 the number of passengers carried by the world's airlines increased threefold. Only "jumbo jets" could prevent the skies becoming overcrowded.

1930	Douglas DC–3 (Dakota)
1940	Martin Clipper
1950	Lockheed Constellation
	Boeing 727
1960	Boeing 747
1970	

0   50   100   150   200   250   300   350

Millions of Passengers

The above diagram shows how the size of airliners has grown over the past 40 years.

The idea of "stretching" an airliner and fitting more seats was first thought of in the 1950s. As more powerful engines were developed airliners grew larger. The Russians produced huge turboprop transports like the Tu–114 and the An–22. But the turboprop plane was soon replaced on long range flights by the faster jets. The first successful jetliners were the Boeing 707 and the Douglas DC–8.

When the 707 first entered service in 1958 many people believed it would fail. No airline, they believed, would fill the 707's 130

Above: The Lockheed C-5A Galaxy is the world's largest aircraft. It has 28 landing wheels and huge doors at the nose and tail open to allow cargo to be loaded. It was designed as a military transport, and can carry 265,000 pounds of men and materials over 2875 miles at 530 mph.

seats. Yet by the 1960s the 707 had been "stretched" to carry 189 passengers. And the DC–8 was soon stretched in the "Super Sixty" series to seat 250 passengers.

Even so, these aircraft could not cope with the growing number of air travelers. Even larger planes were needed to cope with the numbers and also to reduce the amount of traffic in and out of airports.

The Boeing 747

The first "jumbo jet" was the Boeing 747 which went into airline service with Pan American in 1970. It was a huge aircraft, weighing twice as much as any previous airliner. Each of its four engines produced 43,500 pounds of thrust (compared with the 18,000 pounds of thrust of the most powerful engines used in the 707).

The Boeing 747 can carry up to 490 passengers. Its huge cabin is 20 feet wide and 185 feet long, with headroom of over eight feet. But the basic passenger model seats only 374 people and is very comfortable.

Above: The cabins of the "jumbo" jets give plenty of room for all the passengers. The upper picture shows the first class cabin of a 747. The lower picture shows the coach class comfort of a TriStar.

Left: The Boeing 747 is 231 feet long and has a wing span of just over 195 feet. It flies at around 600 miles an hour. The hump at the front of the fuselage holds the flight deck and an upstairs lounge.

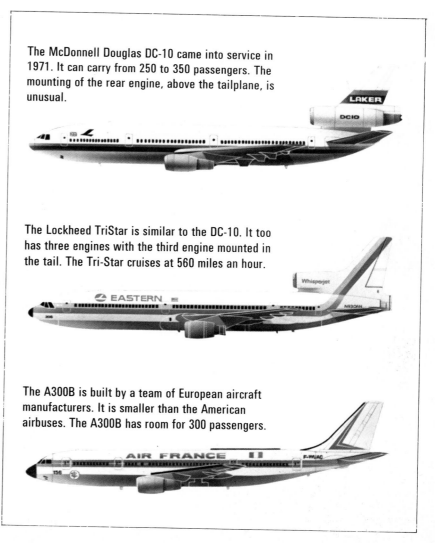

The McDonnell Douglas DC-10 came into service in 1971. It can carry from 250 to 350 passengers. The mounting of the rear engine, above the tailplane, is unusual.

The Lockheed TriStar is similar to the DC-10. It too has three engines with the third engine mounted in the tail. The Tri-Star cruises at 560 miles an hour.

The A300B is built by a team of European aircraft manufacturers. It is smaller than the American airbuses. The A300B has room for 300 passengers.

lems at airports when large numbers of passengers arrive at the same time from one aircraft. Nevertheless, the jumbo jets have proved reliable in service and popular with passengers.

Before the arrival of the jumbo, jet airliners seemed almost cramped. The 747 introduced the idea of two passenger compartments, one above the other, connected by stairs. This "double decker" layout was used on one of the last and most popular of the big piston-engined airliners, the Boeing Stratocruiser.

The Airbuses

After the Boeing 747 came the airbuses, – the McDonnell Douglas DC–10 and the Lockheed L–1011 TriStar. These aircraft work economically over short and medium distances. They are wide bodied jets, carrying six or more passengers abreast. Both are three engined aircraft, with one turbofan mounted beneath each wing and the third at the tail. They can carry more than 300 passengers.

The A–300B is a European airbus built by a team of European aerospace firms as a cooperative venture. It is smaller than the DC–10 and TriStar and has only two engines. The A–300B is designed to operate when large numbers of passengers need to be carried over shorter distances – as between European cities.

Beyond the Jumbo Jets

The Boeing 747 could be "stretched" to carry as many as 700 passengers. Airliners able to carry 1,000 passengers are not more than a few years away. But the jumbo jets have brought other problems. They were designed when air traffic was increasing steadily. But economic troubles have affected airline business and often the jumbos have flown with far less than their full passenger load. The size of the aircraft has also created prob-

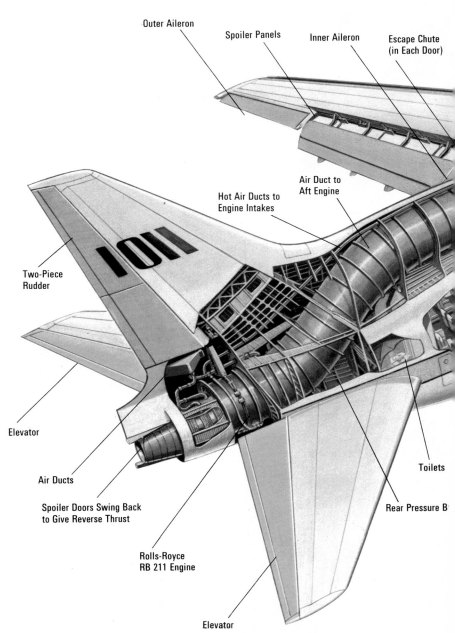

Outer Aileron
Spoiler Panels
Inner Aileron
Escape Chute (in Each Door)
Air Duct to Aft Engine
Hot Air Ducts to Engine Intakes
Two-Piece Rudder
Elevator
Air Ducts
Spoiler Doors Swing Back to Give Reverse Thrust
Rolls-Royce RB 211 Engine
Toilets
Rear Pressure B
Elevator

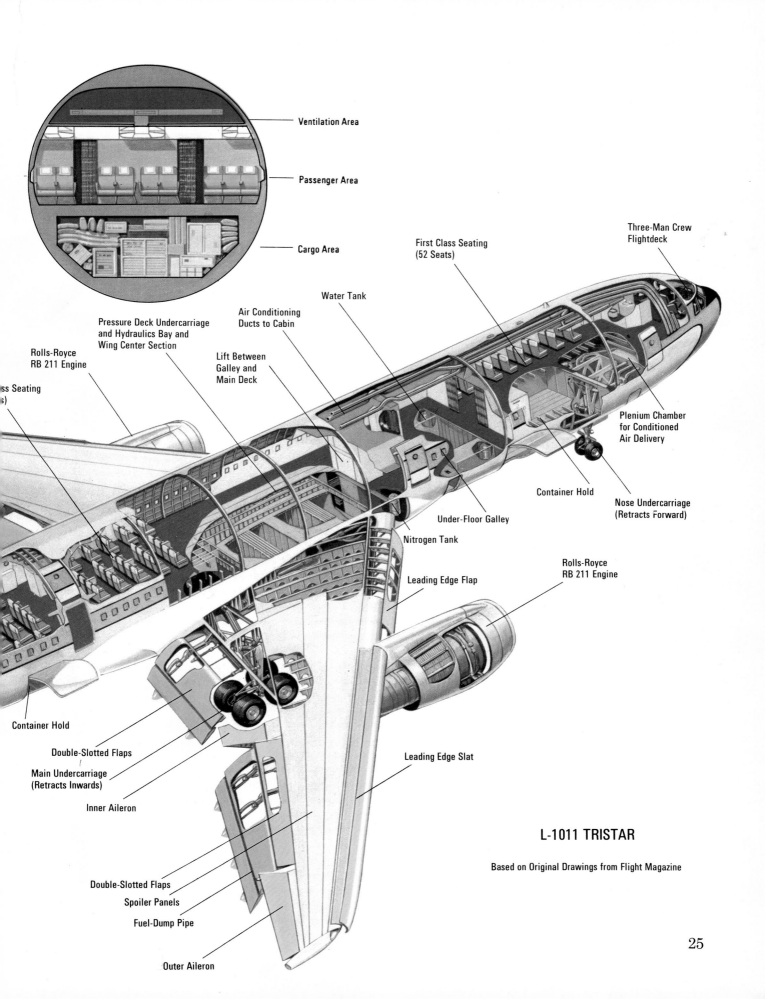

Ventilation Area

Passenger Area

Cargo Area

First Class Seating
(52 Seats)

Three-Man Crew
Flightdeck

Water Tank

Pressure Deck Undercarriage
and Hydraulics Bay and
Wing Center Section

Air Conditioning
Ducts to Cabin

Rolls-Royce
RB 211 Engine

Lift Between
Galley and
Main Deck

Plenium Chamber
for Conditioned
Air Delivery

ss Seating
s)

Container Hold

Under-Floor Galley

Nose Undercarriage
(Retracts Forward)

Nitrogen Tank

Leading Edge Flap

Rolls-Royce
RB 211 Engine

Container Hold

Double-Slotted Flaps

Leading Edge Slat

Main Undercarriage
(Retracts Inwards)

Inner Aileron

L-1011 TRISTAR

Based on Original Drawings from Flight Magazine

Double-Slotted Flaps

Spoiler Panels

Fuel-Dump Pipe

Outer Aileron

Supersonic Flight

In 1947 a young American pilot, Charles Yeager, tried to break through the invisible "sound barrier" in the rocket-powered Bell X-1. His plane was battered by shock waves as it approached the speed of sound. Suddenly the violent shuddering stopped. Supersonic flight had been achieved.

Concorde taking off. Its slim delta wing shape is ideal for supersonic flight. Concorde has a maximum cruising speed of 1,450 miles an hour at heights above 54,000 feet.

Supersonic flight is flight faster than the speed of sound. This speed is 760 miles an hour at sea level. But at heights above about 36,000 feet, it is only 660 miles an hour. An aircraft traveling at the speed of sound, whatever its height, is said to be traveling at Mach 1. Twice the speed of sound is Mach 2, and so on.

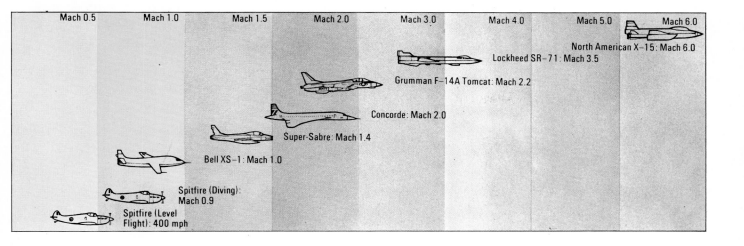

Mach 0.5   Mach 1.0   Mach 1.5   Mach 2.0   Mach 3.0   Mach 4.0   Mach 5.0   Mach 6.0

North American X–15: Mach 6.0

Lockheed SR–71: Mach 3.5

Grumman F–14A Tomcat: Mach 2.2

Concorde: Mach 2.0

Super-Sabre: Mach 1.4

Bell XS–1: Mach 1.0

Spitfire (Diving): Mach 0.9

Spitfire (Level Flight): 400 mph

The Sound Barrier

During World War II, pilots of fighter aircraft had difficulty when diving at high speeds. It felt as if their plane were flying into a wall of air. The aircraft shook wildly, and was difficult to control. Some aircraft broke up in mid air.

The reason for this buffeting was that the aircraft was flying so fast that the air in front could not get out of the way. Instead of flowing smoothly past the aircraft, the air built up in front of it as "shock waves". These shock waves caused the buffeting and also put the aircraft under strain. The first jet aircraft came up against this so-called "sound barrier". And there were fears that this invisible barrier might be impossible to break.

But experiments with models in wind tunnels showed that the sound barrier could be broken through. A streamlined plane reduced the buffeting. Swept-back wings were better than straight wings. Jet aircraft were made that could travel safely at supersonic speed. The first plane to fly faster than sound was the rocket-powered Bell X–1 in 1947.

Nowadays fighters can fly faster than Mach 2 (1,500 miles an hour). Types such as the Lockheed SR–71 can fly at Mach 3 (more than 2,000 miles an hour). The rocket-powered North American X–15 reached speeds of Mach 6 (4,500 miles an hour) during the 1960s.

Sonic Boom

As it passes through the sound barrier, an aircraft makes shock waves before it. These shock waves can be heard on the ground as a "sonic boom". The waves can also cause damage to buildings. Both the Russian Tu–144 and Anglo-French Concorde airliners can fly at more than 1,450 miles an hour. But because of the sonic boom, they will not fly at speeds faster than sound over populated areas. During the 1970s, however, the age of the supersonic airliner will bring huge cuts in traveling time on long-distance flights. It will indeed seem as if the world has shrunk.

Above: the invention of the jet engine brought a rapid increase in the speed of aircraft. The Bell X-1 reached Mach 1 in 1947. The F-100 Super Sabre was the first true supersonic fighter at Mach 1·4. The X-15 has reached Mach 6.

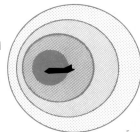

Below Mach 1 an aircraft flies inside pressure waves caused by its motion through the air. But the waves, traveling at the speed of sound stay well ahead of the plane.

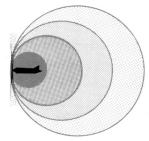

As Mach 1 is reached, the plane catches up with the pressure waves. They build up to form a shock wave.

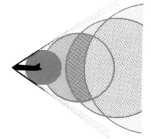

Above Mach 1 the plane is traveling so fast that it leaves the pressure waves behind. The shock wave bends back.

Vertical Take off

Long concrete runways may one day be a thing of the past at many airports. Jump jets may be used to carry passengers.

The Rolls-Royce Pegasus II engine is used in the Harrier. The Pegasus engine has four rotating nozzles which can be moved so as to give rearward thrust for normal forward flight or downward thrust for take off.

As the size of airliners has increased, airports too have grown larger. Land close to the center of cities is scarce and expensive, so airports are often built many miles away. This means a long road or rail journey for the passengers – sometimes taking as long as the flight itself. It would be simpler if airliners could land in the heart of the city. But a plane cannot land on a small area. It must have a long concrete runway. The answer is a plane which can rise straight up in the air and land in the same way. This is called vertical take off and landing (VTOL).

A helicopter can take off vertically, hover and land on almost any level patch of ground. But it cannot lift such heavy loads as a fixed wing aircraft. And it cannot fly as fast. The VTOL aircraft must be able to take off and land vertically (or in a very short distance). Then it must fly forward like an ordinary plane.

Several VTOL planes were tried during the 1950s and 1960s. Often they were strange looking machines. Some had tilting wings. Others had engines which swiveled, or fixed jet engines pointing downwards. They were clumsy and often difficult to fly. Air forces were interested in VTOL because such aircraft could operate from any small rough airstrip.

The great advantage of the "jump jets" is that they can operate from small airfields. The Harrier, for example, can land on a makeshift runway in the middle of a forest.

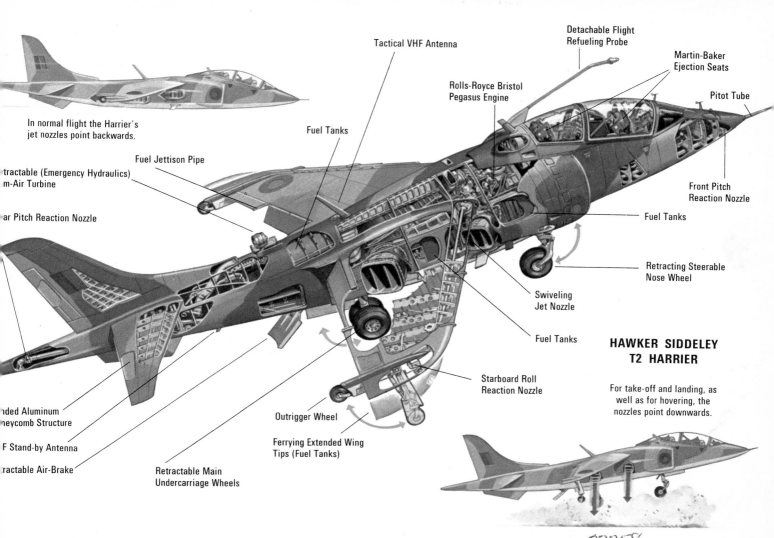

In normal flight the Harrier's jet nozzles point backwards.

Tactical VHF Antenna

Detachable Flight Refueling Probe

Rolls-Royce Bristol Pegasus Engine

Martin-Baker Ejection Seats

Pitot Tube

Fuel Tanks

Retractable (Emergency Hydraulics) Ram-Air Turbine

Fuel Jettison Pipe

Front Pitch Reaction Nozzle

Rear Pitch Reaction Nozzle

Fuel Tanks

Retracting Steerable Nose Wheel

Swiveling Jet Nozzle

Fuel Tanks

HAWKER SIDDELEY T2 HARRIER

For take-off and landing, as well as for hovering, the nozzles point downwards.

Banded Aluminum Honeycomb Structure

Starboard Roll Reaction Nozzle

UHF Stand-by Antenna

Outrigger Wheel

Retractable Air-Brake

Ferrying Extended Wing Tips (Fuel Tanks)

Retractable Main Undercarriage Wheels

Many early VTOL aircraft were strange machines. The Rolls-Royce "flying bedstead" was used to test downward-pointing jets for vertical take-off and landing.

The first successful VTOL plane was a warplane – the Hawker Siddeley Harrier. It is now being used by the Royal Air Force and the United States Marine Corps. The Harrier's turbofan engine has four nozzles. These can be turned to direct the engine's thrust downwards to raise the aircraft from the ground or backwards for normal forward flight. The Harrier can hover and fly backwards. Yet it can reach almost supersonic speed in level flight.

But no large passenger-carrying VTOL aircraft has so far been built. Several designs are being considered, however. In the crowded skies of tomorrow such an aircraft will be very useful.

A halfway step before the true VTOL "jump jet" is a plane which can take off and land in short distances (STOL). This is an aircraft which can operate from very short runways. At present the most useful STOL types are fairly small aircraft. These planes have a high wing which gives greater lift.

"Jump jets" are likely to play an important part in aviation during the 1970s and 1980s. Airliners faster than today's Concorde will be expensive to build and operate. Airliners very much larger than the present day "jumbos" may not be profitable. Smaller VTOL and STOL airliners, able to carry passengers cheaply to and from cities, are likely to play an important part in the future.

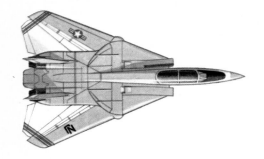

The Swing-Wing

As early as 1918 it was said that the ideal airplane should be able to change its wing area in flight. The "swing-wing" design has at last made this possible.

The best design for high speed flight is a thin, swept-back wing which cuts down drag. But even the fastest aircraft must land and take off at slower speeds. This is where the swept-back wing is less successful. It gives less drag, but it also gives less lift. For low speed flight the ideal wing is one with its front edge almost at right angles to the fuselage.

After years of study the "swing-wing" was invented. For take-

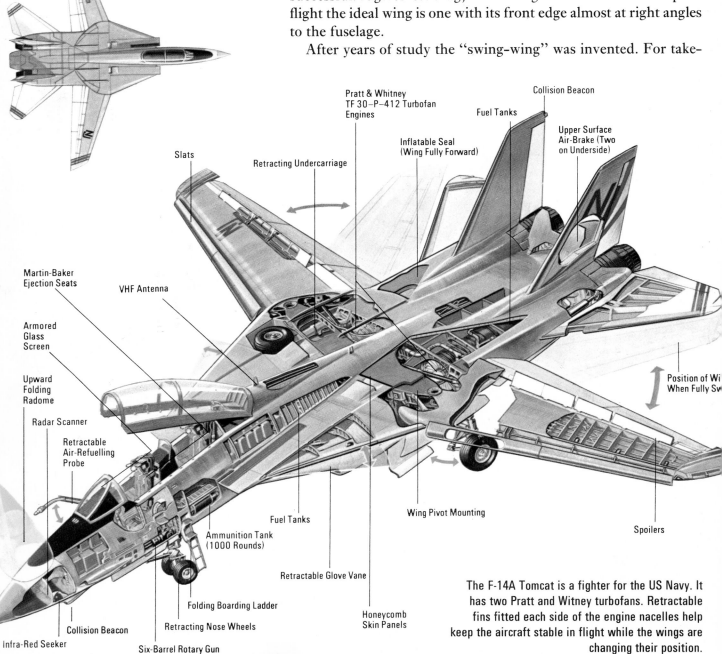

Pratt & Whitney
TF 30–P–412 Turbofan
Engines

Collision Beacon

Fuel Tanks

Inflatable Seal
(Wing Fully Forward)

Upper Surface
Air-Brake (Two
on Underside)

Slats

Retracting Undercarriage

Martin-Baker
Ejection Seats

VHF Antenna

Armored
Glass
Screen

Upward
Folding
Radome

Radar Scanner

Retractable
Air-Refuelling
Probe

Position of Wi
When Fully Sw

Fuel Tanks

Wing Pivot Mounting

Spoilers

Ammunition Tank
(1000 Rounds)

Retractable Glove Vane

Folding Boarding Ladder

Retracting Nose Wheels

Honeycomb
Skin Panels

Collision Beacon

Infra-Red Seeker

Six-Barrel Rotary Gun

The F-14A Tomcat is a fighter for the US Navy. It has two Pratt and Witney turbofans. Retractable fins fitted each side of the engine nacelles help keep the aircraft stable in flight while the wings are changing their position.

F-111A

The General Dynamics F-111A was the first swing-wing aircraft. The aircraft is shown here with its wings midway between the "closed-up" delta shape used for high-speed flight and the "straight-wing" position for low speed flight. The F-111A has a maximum speed of 1,650 miles an hour and first flew in 1964.

B-1

The North American Rockwell B-1 bomber is about the size of a Boeing 707. The B-1 has a top speed higher than Mach 2 and a maximum range of over 6000 miles. It has four General Electric F101 supersonic turbofan engines.

The small foreplanes on the nose are designed to steady the plane in high-speed, low-level flight.

MRCA

The Panavia MRCA is a joint European design for a two-seat, swing-wing warplane. It is shown with the wings swept back for high-speed flight. Some 900 of these planes are to be built for the air forces of Britain, West Germany and Italy. They are expected to enter service in 1977. The MRCA will be able to fly at speeds above Mach 2 at great heights.

Birth of the Swing-Wing

The idea of swing-wing aircraft came from the British scientist Dr. Barnes Wallis. Dr. Wallis designed a swing-wing airliner called the Swallow. But this never got beyond the drawing-board. The idea of altering an aircraft's shape while it is in the air by moving the wings, was first tried in the United States. The first experiments were not too successful. Later swing-wing planes, however, have been successful.

General Dynamics F-111A

North American Rockwell B-1

Panavia MRCA

off, landing and slow-speed flight, the wings are moved forward into a straight-wing shape. This gives greater lift. For high speed flight the wings are moved back to give a swept wing, or "delta" wingshape.

The first plane to be able to adjust its wings in flight was the Bell X–5 in 1951. But the first production model to do this was the General Dynamics F–111A. It first first flew in 1964. The F–111A was the first of several swing-wing aircraft.

Today, the variable sweep wing is an important part of the world's fastest combat planes. These include the Grumman F–14A "Tomcat" and the European Panavia MRCA (Multi-Role Combat Aircraft).

31

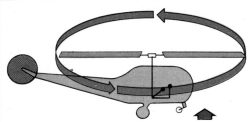

To fly upwards, all the helicopter's rotor blades are kept at the same angle or "pitch".

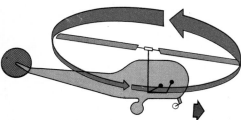

To fly forwards, the rotor blades are tilted forwards. The blades increase their pitch as they move towards the tail and "bite" more air.

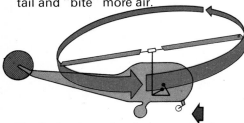

To fly backwards, the opposite happens. The rotor blades are tilted backwards and get more pitch as they move towards the nose.

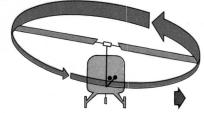

To move sideways, the rotor blades are tilted in the direction the pilot wishes the helicopter to travel. (When turning, the small tail rotor does the work.)

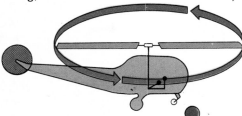

To hover, all the rotor blades are kept at the same pitch. The balance between the helicopter's weight and the rotor's upward pull gives this effect.

Helicopters

The helicopter can take off and land vertically, hover motionless in the air, and even fly backwards.

In ancient times men dreamed of building machines with screw-like propellers on top. These would be able to draw the machines up into the air. Leonardo da Vinci designed such a flying machine. But there was no engine powerful enough to drive it. However, model helicopters were built and flown. The most successful had two rotors (large top propellers) turning in opposite directions. A helicopter with a single rotor is useless. The whole machine spins in the opposite direction to the rotor.

The man-carrying helicopter was not possible until light gasoline engines were made. Several inventors came near to success in the early part of the 20th century. The Breguet brothers, Louis and Jacques, built a helicopter which lifted itself off the ground in 1907. Another French inventor, Paul Cornu, made the first free flight in a helicopter shortly afterwards. But he lacked the money to develop his machine.

In 1928 the autogyro appeared. Designed by the Spaniard Juan de la Cierva, the autogyro had a rotor that was not driven by an engine – it free wheeled. This gave extra lift as the machine moved

The Russian Mil Mi-10 is one of the most powerful helicopters ever built. Heavy loads can be lifted on a special platform beneath the fuselage.

The twin-rotor Boeing-Vertol 107-11 helicopter. Twin rotors are common on larger helicopters.

The German Focke-Wulf FW-61 was the first really successful helicopter. It first flew in 1936.

forward. The autogyro could land and take off in a short distance because of this extra lift.

The first successful helicopter was flown in Germany in 1936. This was the Focke-Wulf FW-61 which had two large rotors. In 1939 Igor Sikorsky produced his VS-300 helicopter. This had a large single rotor and a smaller rotor fixed sideways on the tail. The small rotor stopped the helicopter from spinning round and round. The VS-300 was the first of the modern helicopters.

The Helicopter Today

Since 1945 the use of helicopters has increased rapidly. Helicopters were used in the Korean War and later in Vietnam. They are used to carry troops, to help the wounded, or to carry guns and small vehicles. At sea helicopters are carried aboard ship. They are very useful for anti-submarine work. In peacetime the helicopter has many uses such as air-sea rescue operations, forest fire-fighting, traffic control and, of course, picking up US astronauts from the sea after "splashdown".

When the helicopter first appeared, some people thought that it would replace the motor car. But this has not happened, mainly because helicopters are expensive. There are many jobs that only helicopters can do. However, their low speed prevents them doing the job of fixed-wing aircraft over any distance.

Above: A helicopter landing on the flight deck of an aircraft carrier. Helicopters are used by navies for anti-submarine and rescue duties.

Below: A helicopter of the US Navy hovers while picking up astronauts after splash-down. Helicopters first drop frogmen into the water to secure the floating spacecraft. Then the astronauts are recovered.

The Flightdeck

There are over two hundred controls and instruments on the flight deck of a modern jetliner. Each one is vital to the safety of the aircraft.

The flightdeck of an airliner is in the nose of the plane. Here are the instruments which tell the pilots how the aircraft's systems are working. The array of levers and dials seems bewildering. But each dial and each control is essential to the safety of the aircraft and its passengers and crew.

Flight Controls

Most airliners have two pilots – the captain and his co-pilot – who sit side by side. The main controls for flying an airliner are the same as those in a light plane. There are two sets of main flying controls – the control column and the rudder bar. So each pilot can fly the plane on his own if necessary. During a long flight the pilots hand over control of the aircraft to the automatic pilot. Between the pilots are the throttle levers. These control the engines. Other controls work the landing gear and flaps.

Besides the flight controls, there are three main sets of flight instruments. One set has to do with the working of the engines. These are in the charge of the flight engineer. Another has the navigation instruments which are used by the navigator. The third main set of instruments tell the pilots how the aircraft is flying –

Left: The flight deck of an L-1011. The captain and the co-pilot sit before a bewildering array of instruments. The captain always sits in the left-hand seat. The throttle levers are between the seats. The control column, with its U-shaped hand control, is in front. Above: In the working area of Concorde the flight engineer keeps a check on his instruments.

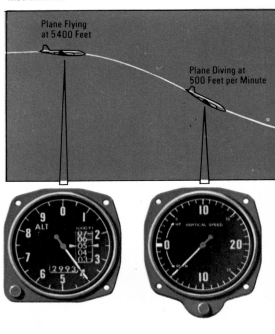

Left: The altimeter, which shows height, is worked by air pressure, like a barometer. The window records height in thousands of feet while the pointer shows hundreds of feet. Right: The vertical speed indicator shows the rate of dive or climb.

Below: The airspeed indicator is worked by air pressure from the pitot-static tube. This is in fact two tubes in one. The open end of the pitot tube sticks forward from the nose or wing of the aircraft. Air rushes in. The indicator measures the difference in pressure between the air rushing into the open pitot tube and the still air inside the enclosed static tube.

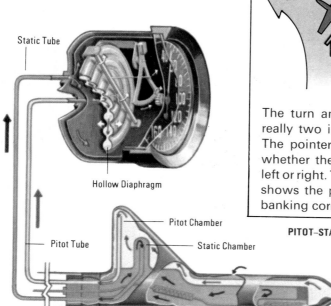

Static Tube

Hollow Diaphragm

Pitot Chamber

Pitot Tube

Static Chamber

Air

Static Holes

PITOT–STATIC TUBE

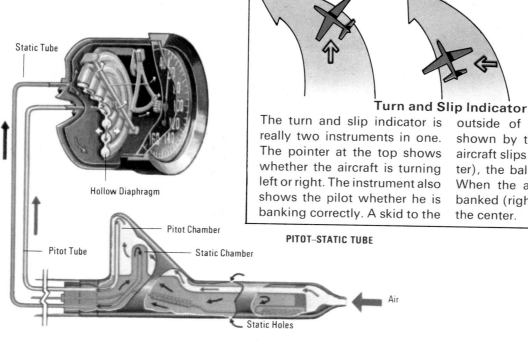

Turn and Slip Indicator

The turn and slip indicator is really two instruments in one. The pointer at the top shows whether the aircraft is turning left or right. The instrument also shows the pilot whether he is banking correctly. A skid to the outside of the turn (left) is shown by the red ball. If the aircraft slips into the turn (center), the ball drops to the left. When the aircraft is correctly banked (right), the ball stays in the center.

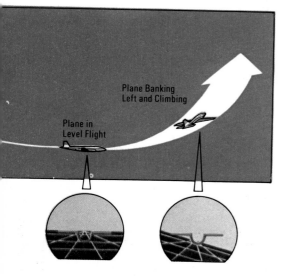

Plane Banking Left and Climbing

Plane in Level Flight

The "artificial horizon" has a bar which remains level with the Earth. In level flight marker and bar are in line. As the "attitude" of the plane changes so does the marker.

whether it is climbing, diving, or turning, whether it is flying straight and level, and so on.

Flight Instruments

The "artificial horizon" shows the pilot immediately if the aircraft is not flying straight and level. The *altimeter* shows the aircraft's height. Some types of altimeter work by changes in air pressure (which is less the higher the aircraft flies); others use radio signals beamed between the plane and ground. The *airspeed indicator* shows the airspeed on a dial. Other important instruments are the *compass* and the *vertical speed indicator*, which is another instrument worked by air pressure. It shows the aircraft's rate of climb or descent. The *turn and slip indicator* tells the pilot if the aircraft is banking (leaning sideways) correctly during a turn. If the bank is not correct, and the plane "slips" away from the turn, this is shown on a dial.

The work of the flight engineer begins before take-off. It is his job to check the aircraft before it takes off and to see that it has enough fuel. During the flight the flight engineer's instruments tell him about the engines and the fuel, the electrical and other systems.

Navigation

Airmen once flew by following roads and railroad tracks. Today there are radio "highways" in the sky.

After an aircraft has taken off it climbs to its cruising height. Then it is set on course at the correct speed. Throughout the flight the pilot must follow the "flight plan" which he is given before take-off. This gives the aircraft's route, course, height, speed and time of arrival at its destination.

At cruising height the pilot can hand over control of the aircraft to the automatic pilot. Automatic pilots are worked by gyroscopes. While the autopilot flies the aircraft at its correct height, the navigating officer is busy with navigation and weather reports.

The navigation officer has many instruments to help him. The modern gyro-compass is very accurate. It shows the direction in which the aircraft is heading. Navigators can also navigate by the stars. But radio and radar navigation is far more common. The radio compass, or automatic direction finder, receives signals from a ground station. Throughout the flight the aircraft is within the range of ground stations. Signals from these help the navigator check and correct his route.

Another device works by sending

An airliner being refueled at an airport. Modern jets need huge amounts of fuel. A Boeing 747 carries a full load of 40,000 gallons. The weight of the fuel at take-off can be more than the weight of the plane itself.

To make sure that his aircraft has enough fuel for the flight the pilot must know how much fuel he will use on each stage of the flight. This will depend on various things – the direction and strength of the winds, the height at which the aircraft flies and the load it is carrying. Allowances must be made for reserves of fuel in case of bad weather or high fuel consumption for any reason. The diagram below shows a typical fuel flight plan.

Sector 1: Climb to 32,000 feet; 33-knot headwind; Fuel consumption 18 kilograms per mile.

Sector 2: Cruise at 32,000 feet; 64-knot headwind reduces speed; Fuel consumption 13 kg per mile.

Sector 3: Cruise at 32,000 feet; 64-knot headwind reduces speed; Fuel load reduced; Fuel consumption 12 kg per mile.

Sector 4: Cruise at 32,000 feet; 47-knot headwind; Fuel consumption 9 kg per mile; Climbing 4,000 feet to a new flight level uses an additional 100 kg.

Sector 5: Cruise at 36,000 feet; 48-knot headwind; Fuel consumption $9\frac{1}{2}$ kg per mile.

Sector 6: Cruise at 35,000 feet; 13-knot headwind and reduced fuel load gives a fuel consumption of $8\frac{1}{2}$ kg per mile.

Sector 7: Descend to 1,000 feet ready to land; 13-knot headwind; Fuel consumption 6 kg per mile.

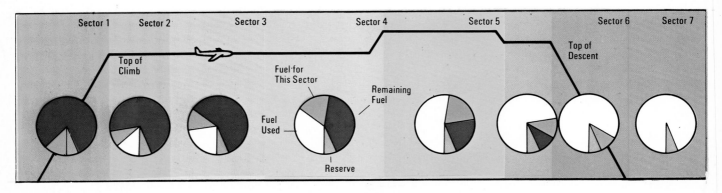

Below: Airmen once flew by following roads, rivers and railroad tracks. Today there are radio "highways" in the sky. The most modern form uses VOR stations. These send out radio signals like the spokes of a wheel. When the pilot tunes in to a VOR station his instruments show him whether he is on course. If the aircraft moves to the right of its course, the pointer moves to the left. The "to-from" indicator (the left-hand circle of each pair) tells the pilot whether he is flying towards the VOR station or away from it.

radio signals from the aircraft down to the ground. The signals "bounce" back to the aircraft and this lets the navigator work out his position. Some guiding systems are operated by radio signals from the ground. One of these is known as VOR.

The navigator must keep track of the aircraft's position all through the flight. This is very important on busy routes where other aircraft are likely to be close. It is even more important if there is an

emergency – a forced landing for instance. Weather conditions affect an aircraft's progress. Head winds reduce the aircraft's speed and tail winds increase it. Side winds can even make the plane drift to the side. Even in bad weather, when the aircraft is flying "blind", the navigator can fix its position on his charts. He can keep the pilot up to date with the aircraft's progress and inform him of any course changes which may be needed.

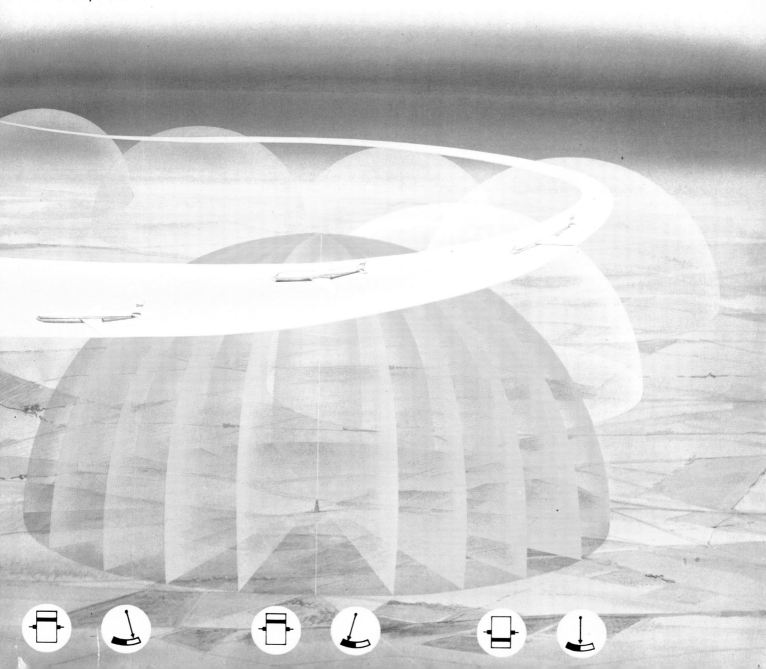

Touchdown

Electronic beams guide huge jet liners to a safe landing on a concrete strip only a few hundred feet wide.

When an airliner nears its destination, it is told by ground control to join a "stack". Aircraft waiting to land are stacked one above the other. They fly in circles, with about 1,000 feet of height between each one. In this way the aircraft are kept well clear of one another. As the plane at the bottom of the stack begins its final approach to land, the plane above comes down to take its place.

Although the plane may have been flying on autopilot throughout its flight, the pilot takes the controls for the landing. The crew check to see that the undercarriage is down and locked and that the flaps are working properly. The air traffic controller at the airport is in radio touch with the pilot. The pilot is told which runway he is to use. Ground control makes sure that all other aircraft are well clear.

Pilots rely on their own skill and experience during touchdown. But various landing aids can help them. One aid is known as VASI (Visual Approach Slope Indicators). The pilot sees a row of colored lights as he approaches the runway. The order in which he sees them tells the pilot whether he is too high or too low.

Lights, of course, are useless in fog. Electronic aids, however, work in all weathers. One method uses radar. Ground control watches the aircraft on a radar screen and passes information to the pilot. This is sometimes called "talking down" an aircraft. Another method is the Instrument Landing System (ILS). This has two radio beams. One is transmitted along the runway. The other is beamed up from the end of the runway at the correct

Above: Radar and other aids keep the air traffic control in touch with all aircraft in their area. In the airport control tower, the control panel shows the position of aircraft on the runways.

On a correct ILS approach to the runway the pointers on the instrument dial are at right angles.

If the aircraft is too far to the left of the glide path, the vertical pointer moves to the right.

Movement of the horizontal pointer shows that the aircraft is too high or too low. Here it is above the glide path.

Stack

angle of approach. This correct approach is known as the "glide path". Instruments on the aircraft show the pilot at once if he is flying to the left or right of the runway beam, or above or below the glide path beam. When the pointers on the instrument dial form a cross the pilot knows he is approaching correctly.

Landing systems can land an aircraft automatically. An automatic landing is possible even in dense fog. But this can only be done at modern airports with the most up-to-date equipment.

After it has touched down on the run-way an aircraft must be slowed quickly and safely. The brakes used are similar to the disk brakes fitted to cars. Each of the aircraft's wheels is fitted with several sets of disks.

The pilot lands the aircraft at the slowest possible safe speed. He uses flaps and airbrakes to cut the airspeed during the final approach. After touchdown he may use "reverse thrust" on the engines to stop more quickly. Many military airplanes, which have high landing speeds, put out a small brake parachute from the tail as they land.

Below: A plane leaves the stack and prepares to land. It is guided by ground control on to the correct glide path. Two radio beacons help the pilot to fix his distance from the runway. Lights flash on the instrument panel as the aircraft passes these markers.

INSTRUMENT LANDING SYSTEM (ILS)

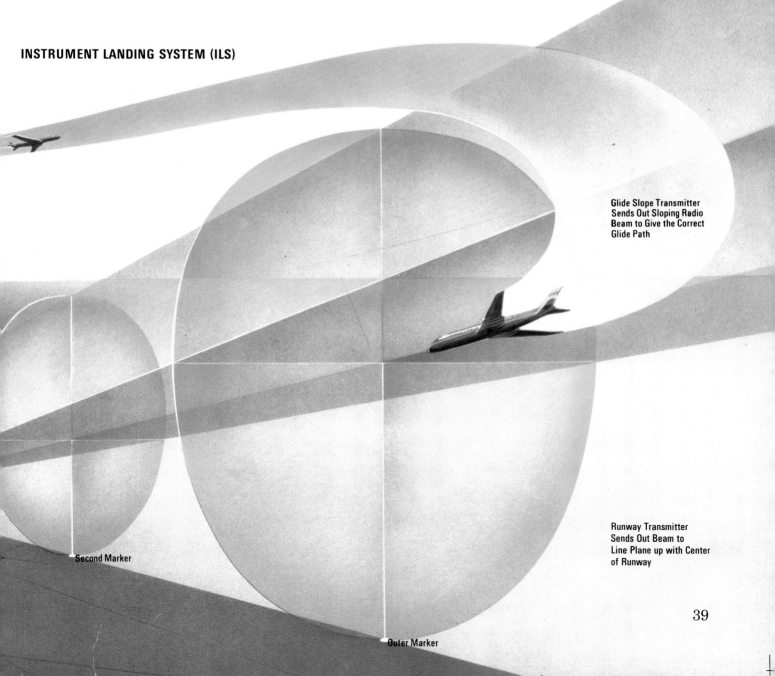

Glide Slope Transmitter Sends Out Sloping Radio Beam to Give the Correct Glide Path

Runway Transmitter Sends Out Beam to Line Plane up with Center of Runway

Second Marker

Outer Marker

Building a New Plane

A modern airliner is a very complicated machine. It is also very reliable.

An aircraft is made up of many thousands of parts. These parts are made separately and the finished pieces put together in the assembly shop. Often the engines come from another country. And sometimes different countries build different parts of the plane. The fuselage and wings are usually made in sections. Then the engines and other systems are fitted. Each part is tested, and when the aircraft is finished a strict test program is carried out before it ever leaves the ground. When all the systems are checked out the plane is ready for its first flight. This marks the start of a further round of flight tests. The first example of a new type of plane, known as a "prototype", is given many tests before it is granted a certificate. These include tests of the radar and navigation systems as well as a flying program to test the aircraft in every kind of situation.

Above: A new design has taken shape in the imagination of the designer. Now, many thousands of drawings have to be made before the aircraft can be built.

Left: Many tests must be made before the first flight of the prototype. Models of the aircraft are made and these are tested in a wind tunnel. Wind tunnel tests show how the aircraft will behave in flight.

Lower Left: Often colored smoke is used to show the flow of air around the model.

Below: A complete airframe of a new plane such as Concorde is made for testing.

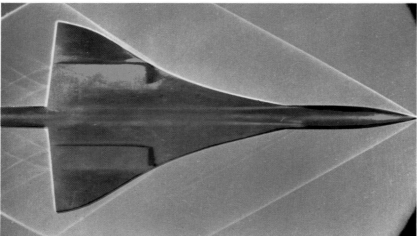

Above: The Concorde production line. Aircraft are in different stages of construction. Sometimes parts are brought from other factories.

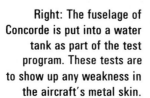

Right: The fuselage of Concorde is put into a water tank as part of the test program. These tests are to show up any weakness in the aircraft's metal skin.

Airlines of the World

To the early airline passenger every flight was an adventure. Today over 300 million people are whisked effortlessly and safely each year to every corner of the world.

Airliners of the 1930s were slow by today's standards. But they offered their passengers a high degree of comfort and service. It was rather like traveling in a rather cramped hotel.

Passenger-carrying air services made a slow beginning after World War I. Passengers wore full flying gear and carried a hot-water bottle in really cold weather. The aircraft used by the early airlines had four instruments and one radio. Bad weather was often a danger. Even rain could result in the stopping of a flight. One flight from London to Paris took over two days, with 20 forced landings on the way. Nevertheless, accidents were rare and the service slowly improved.

During the 1930s great advances were made. Many of the present-day airlines began at this time. Biplanes were replaced by all-metal monoplanes such as the Douglas DC–2 and the Junkers Ju–52. The new aircraft carried more passengers faster and more safely. But they needed concrete runways rather than grass airstrips. One answer was the flying boat, which was used on oversea routes during the 1930s. But the land plane became more reliable and new airports were built. The flying boat was no longer used.

After World War II, airlines had to

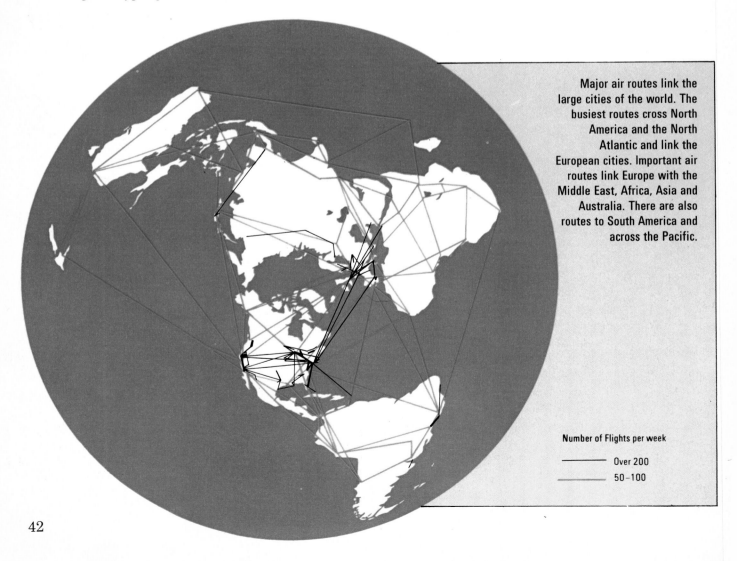

Major air routes link the large cities of the world. The busiest routes cross North America and the North Atlantic and link the European cities. Important air routes link Europe with the Middle East, Africa, Asia and Australia. There are also routes to South America and across the Pacific.

Number of Flights per week

——— Over 200

——— 50–100

rely on old military planes until new civil aircraft were built. The Stratocruiser was a development of the Boeing B-29 bomber; Lancaster bombers were converted for civil use. But soon new planes were in the air. In 1952 the De Havilland Comet, the world's first jetliner, went into service. Turboprop airliners, such as the Vickers Viscount, also came into use, and aircraft such as the Boeing 707, Douglas DC-8 and French Caravelle were sold to airlines.

The jumbo jet allowed airlines to carry many more passengers. In the 1970s the Concorde supersonic airliner made journeys twice as fast as before. The big airlines now offer services to almost every country in the world. The air traveler today enjoys comfort far removed from the bumpy journeys of the 1920s. Cheap rate charter flights have enabled many more people to fly, particularly on vacation.

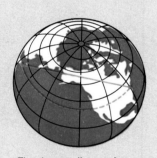

The shortest distance between two points on a globe does not follow the lines of latitude. This can be seen by stretching a piece of string between them. The shortest distance is part of a "great circle"

On an air map great circles are shown as straight lines. The map can have any place as its center. In this case it is New York. A straight line drawn from New York represents the shortest distance from there to any other point on the map.

Aeroflot (AFL): The Soviet state airline is one of the largest in the world, with 350,000 route miles.

Pan American Airways (PAA): Pan American has more than 70,000 miles of air routes.

Air Canada (AC): Another state airline, with 35,000 route miles.

Qantas Airways (QA): The Australian international airline.

Air France (AF): One of the main world airlines, with international and European routes of 200,000 miles.

Royal Dutch Airlines (KLM): The world's oldest operating airline, organized in 1919. More than 160,000 route miles.

American Airlines (AA): One of the largest US air carriers set up in 1934.

Sabena Belgian World Airlines (SAB): Founded in 1923, Sabena has more than 87,000 route miles.

British Overseas Airways Corporation (BOAC): Now part of British Airways, BOAC flies over more than 160,000 route miles.

Scandinavian Airlines (SAS): The airline of Sweden, Norway and Denmark, SAS operates worldwide with more than 130,000 route miles.

Eastern Air Lines (EA): Serves the eastern part of the US, Canada, the Caribbean and South America.

Swissair (SR): A private company with world-wide services.

Japan Air Lines (JAL): Operates a world-wide service and is partly state-owned.

Trans World Airlines (TWA): One of the largest airlines in the US. Organized in 1925.

Lufthansa (LH): The state-aided West German airline is one of Europe's oldest.

United Air Lines (UA): Carries more traffic than any other US airline.

43

Swept Wings,
Engines in Pods
Beneath Wing
(707)

Straight Wings,
Four Turboprop
Engines (Vanguard)

Swept Wings, Engines
at Rear of Fuselage
(One-Eleven)

Delta Wing,
Engines in
Nacelles
Underwing
(Concorde)

Aircraft Recognition

The sky is full of aircraft. Certain features, such as the wing shape, tail design, or the position of the engines, can help to identify a plane.

Aircraft recognition depends largely on spotting one or more of several main features. One of the most important is the shape of the wings. Before the jet age, most aircraft had straight wings. Higher speeds brought in the swept wing. This is now seen in many aircraft. Swept wings reduce buffeting and drag at high speed. But straight wings give better lift at low speed. These two types of wing are combined in "swing-wing" designs. In these the wing shape can be changed in flight, depending on the speed of the aircraft.

The delta wing is perhaps the most easily spotted aircraft shape. Aircraft built to this design include the Concorde supersonic airliner.

Engine Arrangements

The position of the engines is another good way of identifying aircraft. Airliners such as the Boeing 707 and 747 have their engines mounted beneath the wing. To reduce noise in the passenger area, many airliners have their engines mounted at the tail. This fashion was begun by the French Caravelle. Usually rear-engined aircraft have their engines on either side of the fuselage as in the BAC One-Eleven and DC–9. But the designers of the British Trident created a three-jet version with one engine either side of the fuselage and a third mounted in the tail. This layout has been followed in the Boeing 727, the Tu–154 and the Lockheed L–1011 TriStar. The DC–10 is unusual. It has one of its three engines mounted in the fin above the tail plane.

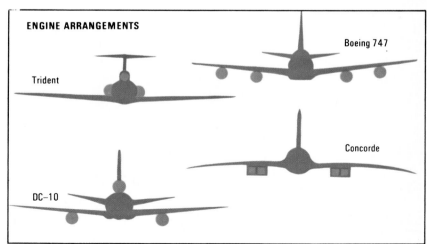

ENGINE ARRANGEMENTS

Trident

Boeing 747

DC–10

Concorde

You often see the Boeing 727. It has a high tailplane with three engines at the rear. There is one either side of the fuselage and one at the base of the fin.

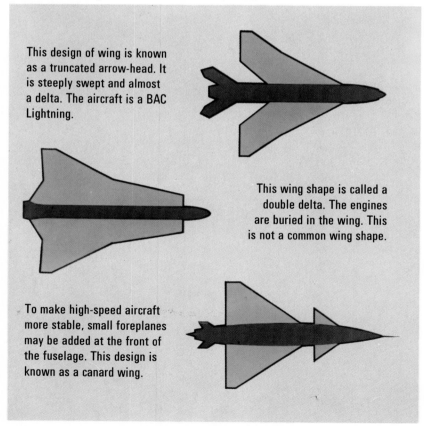

This design of wing is known as a truncated arrow-head. It is steeply swept and almost a delta. The aircraft is a BAC Lightning.

This wing shape is called a double delta. The engines are buried in the wing. This is not a common wing shape.

To make high-speed aircraft more stable, small foreplanes may be added at the front of the fuselage. This design is known as a canard wing.

Rear-engined, high-mounted tailplane (VC-10).

Rear engined (one engine in fin), high tailplane (Boeing 727).

Rear-engined, tailplane midway on fin (Caravelle).

Low mounted tailplane and fin (747).

45

Glossary of Terms

A

Aerobatics. Maneuvers carried out by aircraft in flight, either singly or in formation.

Aerodrome. Another word for an airport or airfield.

Aerodynamics. The study of the forces which act on a flying body, such as an aircraft.

Aerofoil. Part of an aircraft specially shaped to produce lift – such as the wing or tailplane.

Aerospace. The area above and around the Earth in which flight is possible.

Aerostat. A lighter-than-air flying machine, such as an airship or a balloon.

Afterburning. Boosting an aircraft's performance by injecting extra fuel into the jet pipe.

Ailerons. Flaps on the trailing edge of the wing which make the aircraft bank.

Air brakes. Flaps on the wings or fuselage which when extended increase drag and slow down the aircraft.

Airframe. The whole of an aircraft *without* its engines.

Air Intake. Opening through which air is sucked into an aero-engine.

Airplane. A heavier-than-air flying machine with fixed wings and an engine.

Airscrew. Another word for a propeller.

Airship. A lighter-than-air machine powered by an engine.

Airspeed indicator. Instrument which measures the speed of an aircraft.

Air traffic control. Control of aircraft in flight from the ground.

Altimeter. Instrument which measures an aircraft's height above the ground.

Amphibian. An aircraft capable of operating from land or water.

Angle of attack. Angle at which the wing is inclined to the airflow.

Approach lights. Lights marking the approach to an airport runway.

Apron. Concrete area close to airport buildings for the loading and unloading of aircraft.

Arrester gear. Hooks or nets used to halt an aircraft when landing, especially on an aircraft carrier.

Artificial horizon. Instrument which shows the pilot the attitude of his aircraft.

Assisted take off. Using extra power unit (such as rockets).

Autogyro. Aircraft which gets its lift from an unpowered rotor, but which has wings and a propeller. The Autogyro was pioneered by Juan de la Cierva.

Automatic pilot. A device (set by the pilot or ground-controlled) which flies an aircraft automatically.

Auxiliary rotor. Small tail rotor on a helicopter.

Axial-flow turbojet.
Axial-flow turbojet. Typical torbojet engine with from 1 to 3 compressors.

B

Balloon. An unpowered lighter-than-air aircraft.

Banking. Maneuver (used for turning) when aircraft wing is tilted.

Biplane. Airplane with two wings, one above the other.

Brake parachute. Small parachute deployed on landing from an aircraft's tail to act as extra brake.

By-pass turbojet. Advanced engine in which some air is allowed to by-pass the combustion chamber and turbine.

C

Canard. Small horizontal plane at front of aircraft; used on early machines and on modern high-speed jets to aid stability.

Cockpit. Area where the pilot of an aircraft sits, nowadays usually called the flight deck.

Control column. Control which works the elevators and ailerons of an aircraft.

Controlled air space. Area close to an airport in which aircraft waiting to land are controlled.

Cowling. Section which covers engines.

D

Delta wing. Triangular-shaped wing used on high-speed aircraft.

Dihedral. Common wing angle. The tips of the wing are higher than the wing roots.

Dirigible. Early steerable airship.

Ditching. Crash-landing an aircraft at sea.

Doppler. Aircraft navigation system which works by "bouncing" radio beams from the ground.

Drag. Resistance of the air to the movement of an aircraft through it.

Drift. Sideways movement of an aircraft caused by air currents.

Drone. Remote-controlled pilotless aircraft.

Droop snoot. Term used for movable nose, raised for flight and lowered ("drooped") to give better visibility when landing.

E

Ejector seat. System for ejecting the pilot safely from a damaged aircraft and parachuting him to the ground.

Elevator. Hinged horizontal plane on the tail of an aircraft.

Envelope. The "skin" of a balloon or airship.

ETA. Estimated time of arrival.

F

Fatigue test. Test of airframe and engines, often "speeded-up" to simulate years of actual service.

Federal Aviation Administration. The authority that carries out the U.S. Government's responsibilities regarding air safety.

Fin. Fixed vertical stabilizer on the tail of an aircraft.

Flap. Hinged surfaces on the trailing edge of the wing which increase lift or drag and are used to reduce landing speed.

Flight plan. Plan showing details of an aircraft's flight (including destination, route, altitude, airspeed and fuel).

Flight recorder or "black box". Records details of the flight and provides valuable information in the event of a crash.

Float. Buoyancy units fixed to the landing gear of float planes and flying boats.

Flying boat. Aircraft with watertight hull which lands and takes off from water.

Flying wing. Tailless aircraft in which the fuselage is part of the wing.

Fuel tanks. Containers for fuel either within the fuselage or wings, or suspended beneath them as "drop-tanks".

Fuselage. The body of an airplane.

G

Gas bag. Gas container within the envelope of a balloon or airship.

Glide path. Line of approach of an aircraft to the airport runway.

Glider. Unpowered airplane.

Ground Controlled Approach (GCA). Radar-controlled system for guiding an aircraft about to land.

Ground controller. Man who controls aircraft movements by radio and radar from the ground.

Guided weapons. Missiles carried by military aircraft. Missiles may be air-to-air or air-to-ground.

H

Hangar. Building in which aircraft are kept.

Helicopter. Aircraft which gets its lift from powered rotating blades or "rotors".

High-pressure compressor. The last compressor through which air passes in a turbojet engine.

Holding pattern. Course (usually oval) flown by an aircraft awaiting clearance to land.

Holding point. Zone marked by a radio beacon at which a ground controller may hold aircraft waiting to land.

I, J, K

ICAO. The International Civil Aviation Organization, world governing body for civil aviation. Headquarters: Montreal in Canada.

Instrument Landing System (ILS). System of landing using radio transmitters and beacons on the ground and special receivers and lights in the aircraft.

JATO. Abbreviation for jet-assisted take-off.

Jet propulsion. Propulsion by reaction from the emission of a jet of air at high speed.

L

Landing direction indicator. T-shaped indicator to show pilots in which direction they should land and take-off.

Leading edge. The front edge of the wing.

Letting down. Losing height in preparation for landing.

Loop. Aerobatic maneuver in which the aircraft makes a complete upwards circle, flying upside-down in the process.

Low pressure compressor. In a turbojet engine with two or more compressors this is the first compressor.

M

Mach number. Measurement of airspeed in relation to the speed of sound (known as Mach 1).

Mock-up. Full-scale model of an aircraft built before construction of a prototype.

Monocoque. Construction technique in which the skin of the fuselage carries the structural load.

Monoplane. Airplane with one wing.

Mooring tower. Mast to which airships were moored.

N, O, P

Nacelle. Streamlined compartment on the outside of the fuselage housing engines or equipment (radar, for example).

Navigation lights. Lights shown by an aircraft at night. Red (port), green (starboard) and white (tail, above and below fuselage) lights flash when the aircraft is in a busy area.

Pancake landing. A landing from too steep an angle at too low a speed.

Parachute. Umbrella-shaped device for slowing aircraft on landing and permitting pilots to descend safely to earth.

Payload. The economic load (passengers, freight) that an aircraft can carry.

Pitching. Movement of an aircraft along its longitudinal axis.

Pitot tube. Used to measure airspeed, this tube measures air entering at speed and also static air surrounding it.

Precision Approach Radar (PAR). Radar system used during landing.

Pressure suit. Worn by pilots of aircraft flying at extreme altitude.

Pressurization. Artificial maintenance of normal air pressure inside an aircraft.

Prototype. First example of a new aircraft.

Pusher. Airscrew pointing backwards which "pushes" the aircraft forwards.

R

Radial engine. Aero engine in which the cylinders are arranged in a circle around the crankshaft.

Ram jet. Simple form of jet engine.

RATOG. Rocket-assisted take-off.

Reheat. See afterburning.

Reverse thrust. Directing jet thrust *forwards* to slow down an aircraft.

Rigid airship. Airship in which the envelope is supported by a metal framework.

Roll. Aerobatic maneuver in which the aircraft rotates around its longitudinal axis.

Rotor. An aerofoil which produces lift by rotating or spinning. Used by helicopters.

Rotor-tip jets. Small jets on the tips of rotor blades.

Rudder. Hinged vertical plane on the tail, which controls the turn to left or right.

Rudder bar. Foot control which works rudder.

Runway. Strip of concrete or tarmac on which aircraft land. Runway numbers are one-tenth the magnetic compass heading to the nearest whole number.

S

Sailplane. Glider able to fly for long periods in air currents.

SARAH. (Search and rescue and homing.) Radar transmitter on a pilot's life jacket.

Seaplane. Airplane able to take-off and land from water, usually fitted with floats.

Semi-rigid. Airship whose envelope is only partly supported by metal framework.

Shroud line. Cord attaching a parachute to its wearer or to a load.

Sonic boom. Noise produced by aircraft traveling at supersonic speed and caused by shock waves.

Sound barrier. Term coined in 1940s for buffeting and other phenomena experienced just below supersonic speed.

Spoiler. Device for reducing or "spoiling" lift, in order to reduce landing speed of an aircraft.

Spin. Aerobatic maneuver in which the aircraft spirals downwards.

SST. Supersonic transport i.e. Concorde.

Stand-off bomb. Powered bomb designed to be released far from its target.

Stall. A stall occurs when an aircraft does not have enough lift and loses height rapidly.

Static line. Line joining a parachute pack to the aircraft, so that when the parachutist jumps the parachute opens automatically.

STOL. Short take-off and landing.

Swing-wing. See variable geometry.

T

Tail. Sometimes called the empennage, consists of the horizontal and vertical stabilizers and control surfaces at the rear of the fuselage.

Test pilot. Pilot who flies new aircraft on test.

Thermal. Current of rising air used by gliders.

Three-point landing. Normal landing when all wheels touch down at the same time.

Thrust. Force produced by aero engines which drives aircraft forwards.

Tractor. Airscrew at the front which "pulls" an aircraft through the air.

Trailing edge. The rear edge of the wing.

Tricycle undercarriage. Landing wheels positioned at nose and under each wing.

Trim. The stable condition of an aircraft in flight.

Triplane. Early airplane with three wings.

Turbofan. Turbojet engine which has a fan added to increase the air supply.

Turbojet. Typical form of pure jet engine.

Turboprop. Jet engine in which the hot exhaust gases provide jet thrust and also drive a conventional propeller.

Turn and slip indicator. Instrument which records turns, skids and slips.

U, V

Undercarriage. Landing gear of an aircraft, usually retracted into the wings and fuselage during flight.

Variable geometry. Aircraft design which permits the wing-shape to be altered in flight. Hence "swing-wing".

Vectored thrust. System of movable nozzles used to deflect jet thrust for vertical take-off.

Ventral tank. Fuel tank carried below the fuselage.

Visual Approach Slope Indicator (VASI). A system of red, green and amber lights on each side of a runway to aid pilots.

VOR. Short for very high frequency omnidirectional range receiver. Navigational aid for pilots flying overland.

VTOL. Vertical take-off and landing.

W, X, Y, Z

Warping. Early system of aircraft steering involving twisting wing-tips.

Winch launch. Method of launching a glider using a stationary winch.

Wind sock. Cone-shaped sleeve which shows the direction of wind on an airfield.

Wind tunnel. Research apparatus in which a model aircraft can be tested in an airstream.

Wing. The main supporting surface of an airplane.

Yaw. Rotation of an aircraft about its vertical axis.

Index